Grammar and Writing 7

Teacher Packet

Answer Keys and Tests

First Edition

Christie Curtis

Mary Hake

Houghton Mifflin Harcourt Publishers, Inc.

Grammar and Writing 7

First Edition

Teacher Packet
Answer Keys and Tests

ISBN-13: 978-1-4190-9856-7
ISBN-10:   1-4190-9856-X

Houghton Mifflin Harcourt Publishers, Inc.
181 Ballardvale Street
Wilmington, MA 01887

http://saxonhomeschool.com

Printed in the United States of America.

1 2 3 4 5 6 7 8 862 16 15 14 13 12 11 10 09

Writing 7 Table of Contents

To the Teacher

We offer the following suggestions to help you implement the program effectively.

Beginning Class

Notice that each lesson begins with a Dictation or Journal Entry, which students will find in the appendix of their textbooks. To begin their grammar/writing period, students need not wait for teacher instruction, for they will know what to do each day:

Monday:	Copy the dictation to prepare for Friday's test.
Tuesday:	Write on a journal topic.
Wednesday:	Write on a journal topic.
Thursday:	Write on a journal topic.
Friday:	Look over dictation to prepare for dictation test.

Dictations

On the first school day of each week, students copy a dictation to study throughout the week for a test on Friday. Note the number of words and punctuation marks in the dictation and discuss grammar concepts found in it. To test your students at the end of the week, read the dictation aloud slowly and clearly, allowing time for your students to write the passage with correct spelling and punctuation.

Journal Topics

On Tuesday, Wednesday, and Thursday (non-dictation days), students will spend approximately five minutes writing on a journal topic. We suggest that the student write on these topics in the order they are listed.

Grammar Lessons

Because of the incremental format of this program, **lessons should be taught in order.** Please do not skip any lessons. After reading a lesson, the students will practice the new concept from that lesson. **Guide students through the questions in the Practice section and check their answers before they begin the Review set.** Some lessons have "More Practice," which is optional. Some students may need it; others will not.

Grammar Test and Writing Day

We suggest that you give a grammar test after every five lessons. (Notice that the first test follows Lesson 10.) The short, twenty-question test should allow time for a Writing Lesson, to be completed on test day, although you may prefer to teach the Writing Lessons on days other than on test days. Please remember that Writing Lessons are sequenced and should be taught in order. The program is designed so that you do not have a grammar lesson to teach on test day. In addition, for the following two or more days you may teach Writing Lessons instead of Grammar in order to allow students to complete the writing project they began on test day.

On the next page is a suggested schedule for teaching Grammar Lessons and Writing Lessons. Some students might need to spend more than one day on a difficult lesson, so be flexible.

Seventh Grade Grammar & Writing Schedule

School Day	Grammar Lesson	Writing Lesson	School Day	Grammar Lesson	Writing Lesson	School Day	Grammar Lesson	Writing Lesson
1	1		49	40		96	76	
2	2		50	test 7	9	97	77	
3	3		51	41		98	78	
4	4		52	42		99	79	
5	5		53	43		100	80	
6	6		54	44		101	test 15	21
7	7		55	45		102		22
8	8		56	test 8	10	103		23
9	9		57		11	104	81	
10	10		58	46		105	82	
11	test 1	Review Lesson	59	47		106	83	
12	11		60	48		107	84	
13	12		61	49		108	85	
14	13		62	50		109	test 16	24
15	14		63	test 9	12	110		25
16	15		64	51		111		26
17	test 2	1	65	52		112	86	
18		2	66	53		113	87	
19		3	67	54		114	88	
20	16		68	55		115	89	
21	17		69	test 10	13	116	90	
22	18		69	56		117	test 17	27
23	19		70	57		118	91	
24	20		71	58		119	92	
25	test 3	4	72	59		120	93	
26	21		73	60		121	94	
27	22		74	test 11	14	122	95	
28	23		75		15	123	test 18	28
29	24		76		16	124	96	
30	25		77	61		125	97	
31	test 4	5	78	62		126	98	
32	26		79	63		127	99	
33	27		80	64		128	100	
34	28		81	65		129	test 19	29
35	29		82	test 12	17	130	101	
36	30		83	66		131	102	
37	test 5	6	84	67		132	103	
38		7	85	68		133	104	
39	31		86	69		134	105	
40	32		87	70		135	test 20	30
41	33		88	test 13	18	136	106	
42	34		89		19	137	107	
43	35		90	71		138	108	
44	test 6	8	91	72		139	109	
45	36		92	73		140	110	
46	37		93	74		141	test 21	31
47	38		94	75				
48	39		95	test 14	20			

Topical Table of Contents

Capitalization

Punctuation

Sentence Structure

Eight Parts of Speech

Verbs

Nouns

Usage

Spelling Rules

Diagramming

Practice and Review Set
Answer Key

LESSON 1 — Four Types of Sentences

Practice 1

a. exclamatory
b. declarative
c. imperative
d. interrogative
e. declarative
f. adopt
g. adapt
h. adept

Review Set 1

1. capital
2. statement
3. thought
4. exclamatory
5. command
6. interrogative
7. sentence
8. exclamatory
9. period
10. question
11. interrogative
12. declarative
13. declarative
14. exclamatory
15. declarative
16. exclamatory
17. imperative
18. imperative
19. interrogative
20. imperative
21. exclamatory
22. interrogative
23. interrogative
24. declarative
25. adopt
26. adept
27. adapt
28. Readers still enjoy *Aesop's Fables*.
29. Look at that huge bullfrog!
30. Have you read "The Crow and the Pitcher"?

LESSON 2 — Simple Subject • Simple Predicate

Practice 2

a. cow
b. plants
c. reporter
d. You (understood)
e. Do graze
f. are
g. ran
h. macron
i. macrofossils
j. macrocosm

More Practice 2   *See Master Worksheets*

Review Set 2

1. subject
2. verb
3. subject
4. action
5. predicate
6. Aesop
7. You (understood)
8. crow

9. pitcher
10. crow
11. problem
12. beak
13. he
14. water
15. is
16. comes
17. lands
18. overflows
19. has discovered
20. drops
21. rises
22. reaches
23. can drink
24. A smart crow solved a problem.
25. Can you solve problems?
26. I have the perfect solution!
27. Do not break the pitcher.
28. macron
29. adept
30. adapt

LESSON 3 Complete Sentences, Sentence Fragments, and Run-on Sentences

Practice 3

a. run-on sentence

b. sentence fragment

c. complete sentence

d. The engagement ring is worn on the fourth finger. Ancient people believed that a . . . . (*or*) The engagement ring . . . finger, because ancient people believed . . . .

e. Ex: The bride in the long white gown carried flowers.

f. human

g. humane

More Practice 3

1. no
2. yes
3. no
4. no
5. yes
6. no
7. yes
8. no
9. yes (you understood)
10. no
11. yes
12. yes (you understood)
13. no
14. no
15. complete sentence
16. sentence fragment
17. run-on sentence
18. sentence fragment
19. complete sentence
20. run-on sentence
21. We sailed around the world.
22. The ship was approaching an iceberg.
23. The ice-covered Arctic Ocean around the North Pole is cold.
24. . . . large masses of ice and packed snow. They form icebergs . . . .
25. The Arctic Ocean is the smallest ocean. It is also the coldest.
26. I saw an iceberg. Did you?

Review Set 3

1. fragment
2. predicate or verb
3. subject
4. complete
5. run-on
6. complete
7. B
8. Shall we look for deeper meanings?
9. This fable has a moral.
10. complete sentence
11. sentence fragment
12. sentence fragment
13. run-on sentence
14. complete sentence
15. you (understood)
16. fox
17. frustration
18. fox
19. We
20. paces
21. lie
22. snarls
23. Do look
24. would taste
25. B
26. B
27. adopt
28. human
29. large
30. adapt

Practice 4

a. lists
b. fed, guarded
c. chewed, gobbled, swallowed, gnawed
d. woman | invented
e. bear | was called
f. microcosm
g. microbus
h. microscope

More Practice 4

1. wrote
2. read
3. writes
4. washed, dried
5. Listen
6. James | swam
7. you | Have swum
8. (you) | Diagram
9. Tom | has been studying
10. Christina | Did pass
11. Omar | had been
12. (you) | Tell

13. <u>Miss Wu</u> | <u>Was teasing</u>

14. <u>I</u> | <u>will adapt</u>

15. <u>Gloria</u> | <u>became</u>

16. <u>Mountains</u> | <u>surrounded</u>

Review Set 4

1. told
2. travels
3. lives
4. eats
5. prepares
6. detests, abhors, loathes
7. crawl, creep, edge, hop
8. pacifies, appeases, calms
9. The crickets' noise bothers the city mouse.
10. To hear horrible screeching sounds is frightening.
11. The city mouse feels uncomfortable in the country.
12. The city mouse finally dozes off. Then, a rooster crows.
13. The city mouse detests the country. The country mouse will visit the city.
14. The carpet . . . mouse. Maybe the city is better than the country.
15. complete sentence
16. sentence fragment
17. run-on sentence
18. imperative
19. exclamatory
20. declarative
21. interrogative

22. <u>cats</u> | <u>Do threaten</u>

23. <u>Bubble gum</u> | <u>sticks</u>

24. <u>streets</u> | <u>smell</u>

25. <u>(you)</u> | <u>listen</u>

26. <u>mouse</u> | <u>Does like</u>

27. subject
28. large
29. Humane
30. small

LESSON 5   **Capitalizing Proper Nouns**

Practice 5

a. Charles Dickens . . . .
b. Uriah Heep . . . Agnes Wickfield . . . .
c. Charles Dickens . . . *A Tale of Two Cities*.
d. . . . Victorian Age, . . . English . . . United States . . . American . . . .
e. . . . English Channel.
f. wave
g. wave
h. waive
i. wave

More Practice 5   *See Master Worksheets*

Review Set 5

1. Henry David Thoreau, Concord, Massachusetts, July
2. Ralph Waldo Emerson, Nathaniel Hawthorne, Boston, Massachusetts
3. Thoreau's, Protestants, France, Catholic

4. Cynthia Dunbar, Thoreau's, British, American Revolutionary War

5. Thoreau, Harvard University, Cambridge, Massachusetts, Charles River

6. Horace Greeley, *New York Herald*

7. Thoreau's, *Walden*

8. Cape Cod, Maine

9. Aunt Yumi, Maple Street

10. Monday

11. waived

12. small

13. human

14. consumes

15. tastes

16. gobble, inhale, nibble, gnaw

17. frightens, terrifies, startles, alarms

18. exclamatory

19. imperative

20. declarative

21. interrogative

22. run-on sentence

23. complete sentence

24. sentence fragment

25. Ex: I learned the meaning of "fair-weather friends."

26. We value our friendships. We might need a friend's help someday.

27. Don't be a "fair-weather friend." A good friend is loyal in good weather and bad.

28. you | Have read

29. crow | sits

30. argument | escalates

Practice 6

a. screeches

b. walks

c. boxes

d. tries

e. plopped

f. bullied

g. knitted

h. placed

i. complied

j. raked

k. slipped

l. batted

m. chewed

n. balked

o. climactic

p. climate

q. climactic

r. climate

Review Set 6

1. supplies

2. fizzes

3. patches

4. hisses

5. yawns

6. cried

7. trapped

8. based

9. talked

10. pried

11. March, Louisa May Alcott, "To the First Robin"

12. *Little Women*, New England

13. Louisa May Alcott's, Orchard House, New England's

14. suffered

15. penned

16. *Answers will vary*. Ex: She did not receive much literary credit during her life.

17. Aesop told a fable. It was about a donkey and a grasshopper. *Or:* Aesop told a fable about a donkey and a grasshopper.

18. sentence fragment

19. complete sentence

20. run-on sentence

21. exclamatory

22. interrogative

23. declarative

24. imperative

25. (you) | eat

26. donkey | will die

27. moral | lies

28. microcosm

29. humane

30. adopt

LESSON 7 — Concrete, Abstract, and Collective Nouns

Practice 7

a. concrete

b. abstract

c. abstract

d. concrete

e. fear, A; paramedic, C; fence, C; lady, C; distress, A

f. Misoneism, A; growth, A; progress, A

g. Mr. Jansen, C; microbus, C; alley, C

h. assortment

i. gaggle

j. bunch

k. misogamist

l. misogynist

m. misoneism

More Practice 7

1. A
2. C
3. A
4. C
5. C
6. A
7. A
8. C
9. C
10. C
11. A
12. C
13. Bryon, C; piano, C; skill, A; enthusiasm, A
14. rhythm, A; zeal, A; John, C; guitar, C
15. Accuracy, A; mathematics, A
16. Henry, C; truth, A; grace, A
17. David, C; integrity, A; friend, C
18. prisoner, C; justice, A; mercy, A
19. clan, herd
20. congregation, team
21. batch, collection, class

Review Set 7

1. notebook, curtain, bench
2. relaxation, consternation

3. litter, bouquet, brood

4. Emily Dickinson, C; poems, C; humor, A; originality, A

5. life, A; unhappiness, A; disappointment, A

6. collection

7. misoneist

8. human

9. climate

10. preaches

11. buzzes

12. muddies

13. talked

14. tried

15. rapped

16. Edward Dickinson, New England Puritans

17. *Springfield Republican*, Emily Dickinson's

18. "I'm Nobody"

19. May, Emily Dickinson, Amherst, Massachusetts

20. lands

21. apologizes

22. . . . any inconvenience. He will . . . .

23. *Answers will vary.* Ex: The gnat is making a formal apology to the bull.

24. run-on sentence

25. compete sentence

26. sentence fragment

27. bull | Does answer

28. you | Have heard

29. declarative

30. interrogative

LESSON 8   Helping Verbs

Practice 8

a. is, am, are, was, were, be, being, been, has, have, had, may, might, must, can, could, do, does, did, shall, will, should, would

b. has served

c. had been elected

d. might have been hoping

e. must have disappointed

f. ally

g. alley

h. alley

i. ally

More Practice 8   *See Master Worksheets*

Review Set 8

1. *Refer to Practice a., above.*

2. was born

3. Shall read

4. must have suffered

5. Did begin

6. might have objected

7. April, *An American Tragedy*, Theodore Dreiser

8. Dreiser, Nobel Prize

9. complete sentence

10. sentence fragment

11. run-on sentence

12. worries

13. misses

14. occurred

15. trapped

16. C

17. A

18. C

19. A

20. collected

21. . . . made of gold. It made . . . . (*or*) . . . made of gold, and it made . . . .

22. swarm, colony

23. declarative

24. interrogative

25. imperative

26. couple | owed

27. goose | was slaughtered

28. ally

29. adapt

30. macrofossil

LESSON 9

Singular, Plural, Compound, and Possessive Nouns • Noun Gender

Practice 9

a. plural

b. singular

c. singular

d. plural

e. briefcase, attorneys-at-law, undergraduate

f. one's

g. rhinoceros's, hunter's

h. bridesmaids', groomsmen's

i. men's, Mom's

j. neuter

k. masculine

l. indefinite

m. feminine

n. orthodontist

o. straight

p. orthotics

q. orthograde

Review Set 9

1. is, am, are, was, were, be, being, been, has, have, had, may, might, must, can, could, do, does, did, shall, will, should, would

2. aliens, autos

3. hot air balloon, soapbox

4. sister-in-law's, brother's, family's

5. "The Mouse and the Frog," Aesop's

6. indefinite

7. feminine

9. neuter

9. masculine

10. will become

11. might extend

12. sun | has risen

13. frog | leaps

14. run-on sentence

15. complete sentence

16. sentence fragment

17. *Answers may vary.* Ex: Now, the drowning mouse is attracting much attention.

18. . . . spies the struggling mouse. The hawk . . . .

19. concrete

20. abstract

21. abstract

22. armada, troop

23. declarative

24. exclamatory

25. alley

26. wave

27. misogynistic

28. catches

29. scurries

30. napped

LESSON 10   **Future Tense**

Practice 10

  a. future tense

  b. past tense

  c. future tense

  d. present tense

  e. shared

  f. shall enjoy

  g. learns

  h. will

  i. shall

  j. Shall

  k. will

  l. statute

  m. stature

  n. statue

  o. stature

More Practice 10   *See "Slapstick Story #1" with Master Worksheets*

Review Set 10

1. caused, past tense

2. chooses, present tense

3. shall read, future tense

4. will convene

5. danced

6. applauds

7. shall

8. will

9. camel, singular

10. beasts, plural; heads, plural

11. camel, indefinite

12. bull, masculine

13. lioness, feminine

14. meeting, neuter

15. camel's

16. downfall

17. is, am, are, was, were, be, being, been, has, have, had, may, might, must, can, could, do, does, did, shall, will, should, would

18. <u>has</u> become

19. name | was

20. Nam | Might have known

21. worked

22. sentence fragment

23. . . . well-known physician. He often treated . . . .

24. O. Henry, concrete; horseshoes, concrete; fun, abstract

25. man, concrete: enjoyment, abstract; books, concrete

26. Tuesday, Gramercy Park, New York, Mr. Bigglesworth, O. Henry

27. Was his life a failure?

28. ortho-

29. hates

30. climax

LESSON 11 — Capitalization: Sentence, Pronoun *I*, Poetry

Practice 11

a. I

b. Fright

c. Everybody
I
Everybody
I'm
Everybody
My
But I

d. bad

e. cacophony

f. cacography

Review Set 11

1. How
How
To
To

2. Shall, I, Aesop's "The Fox and the Mask"

3. A

4. rummages—present tense

5. encountered—past tense

6. Will appear—future tense

7. wishes

8. shall remember

9. lacks

10. mask, singular

11. Looks, plural;
sense, singular

12. mask, neuter

13. fox, indefinite;
wisdom, neuter

14. passes

15. waxes

16. mother-in-law

17. Mr. Smith's

18. is, am, are, was, were, be, being, been, has, have, had, may, might, must, can, could, do, does, did, shall, will, should, would

19. <u>had</u> achieved

20. <u>may</u> <u>have</u> decided

21. Jack London | was

22. pirates | Did steal

23. Jack | had purchased

24. *The expression needs a verb. Answers may vary.* Ex: The tall-masted sailing sloop could sink.

25. French Frank—concrete;
pirate—concrete;
oysters—concrete

26. Youth—abstract;
success—abstract;
Jack London—concrete;
popularity—abstract

27. Do not steal oysters.

28. adept

29. upright

30. statute

LESSON 12 — Irregular Plural Nouns, Part 1

Practice 12

a. confidently

b. confidentially

c. plays

d. ropes

e. donkeys

f. slashes

g. decoys

h. passes

i. tricycles

j. pantries

k. crutches

l. faxes

m. cherries

n. boxes

o. bodies

p. mysteries

q. Larrys

r. Marys

21. Tommys

22. axes

23. finches

24. ponies

25. Debbys

26. misses

27. summaries

28. prefixes

29. suffixes

30. journeys

31. discoveries

32. flies

More Practice 12

1. watches

2. ways

3. countries

4. inches

5. birthdays

6. jellies

7. churches

8. plays

9. Nancys

10. foxes

11. holidays

12. Freddys

13. wrenches

14. delays

15. Montys

16. perches

17. monkeys

18. Allisons

19. grasses

20. blue jays

Review Set 12

1. keys

2. Cindys

3. torches

4. stencils

5. pears, ropes, booths, trees, cots

6. boxes

7. complies

8. paints

9. whipped

10. crashed

11. pried

12. cat's, groom's, ladies', lady's, Wally's

13. sentence fragment

14. Last, Tuesday, I, Louisa May Alcott's, "To (the) First Robin."

15. shall read, future tense

16. live, present tense

17. discussed, past tense

18. torments

19. shall discuss

20. trapped

21. group

22. cat

23. hayloft

24. is, am, are, was, were, be, being, been, has, have, had, may, might, must, can, could, do, does, did, shall, will, should, would

25. mouse | had been thinking

26. . . . many different plans. Then they . . .

27. brilliance

28. confidently

29. confidentially

30. caco-

LESSON 13   Irregular Plural Nouns, Part 2

Practice 13

a. cupfuls

b. brothers-in-law

c. handkerchiefs

d. hooves

e. vermin

f. oxen

g. geese

h. teeth

i. sopranos

j. tomatoes

k. wolves

l. halves

m. euphoria

n. euphony

o. eulogy

More Practice 13

1. thieves

2. wives

3. shelves

4. knives

5. calves

6. feet

7. cacti

8. lice

9. sheep

10. men

11. handfuls

12. women

13. children

14. mice

15. geese

16. cupfuls

17. lives

18. loaves

19. pianos

20. potatoes

21. sisters-in-law

22. gentlemen

Review Set 13

1. cartfuls

2. counselors-at-law

3. portfolios

4. fungi

5. donkeys

6. arches

7. prefixes

8. raspberries

9. feminine

10. masculine

11. neuter

12. devotion, chivalry

13. rinsed

14. cleaned

15. munches

16. fries

17. snipped

18. orthodontists', orthodontist's, sisters', sister's, monkey's

19. Edgar Allen Poe's, "Annabel Lee," It

20. explores

21. will meet

22. amazed

23. army

24. run-on sentence

25. <u>bullfrog</u> | Did grow

26. <u>He</u> | may have exploaded

27. eulogy

28. statute

29. discordant

30. hatred

LESSON 14   Irregular Verbs, Part 1: *Be, Have, Do*

Practice 14

a. is

b. had

c. were

d. was

e. has

f. Does

g. elude

h. allude

i. elude

j. allude

More Practice 14

1. does

2. has

3. were

4. Does

5. were

6. were

7. were

8. are

9. Were

10. Was

11. has

12. Does

13. is

14. is

15. am

16. has

17. have

19. does

20. did

Review Set 14

1. interrogative

2. exclamatory

3. imperative

4. are

5. has

6. does

7. were

8. is

9. had

10. has

11. furnished

12. shall read

13. does

14. ferries

15. tankfuls

16. grottoes

17. roofs

18. hooves

19. turnkeys

20. parches

21. fairies'

22. flipped

23. Edgar Allen Poe's, "The Raven," Once, I

24. company

25. child, indefinite; playground, neuter

26. <u>bus</u> | had been waiting

27. sentence fragment

28. eu-

29. cacophony

30. statue

LESSON 15   **Four Principal Parts of Verbs**

Practice 15

a. (is) honoring, honored, (has) honored

b. (is) crying, cried, (has) cried

c. (is) clipping, clipped, (has) clipped

d. (is) pitching, pitched, (has) pitched

e. (is) substituting, substituted, (has) substituted

f. hypocrisy

g. heresy

h. hypocrisy

More Practice 15

1. (is) pouring, poured, (has) poured

2. (is) adjusting, adjusted, (has) adjusted

3. (is) maltreating, maltreated, (has) maltreated

4. (is) advising, advised, (has) advised

5. (is) learning, learned, (has) learned

6. (is) implying, implied, (has) implied

7. (is) passing, passed, (has) passed

8. (is) allowing, allowed, (has) allowed

9. (is) paring, pared, (has) pared

10. (is) remembering, remembered, (has) remembered

Review Set 15

1. (is) waiving, waived, (has) waived

2. (is) spotting, spotted, (has) spotted

3. am

4. is

5. are

6. Have

7. has

8. Does

9. Do

10. were

11. <u>might</u> <u>have</u> shot

12. <u>will</u> <u>have</u> carried

13. shall critique

14. looks

15. speaks

16. cargoes

17. Ramirezes

18. wolves

19. steamboats

20. A, Bamboo Buffet, Peck Road, El Monte, Chinese

21. antlers', businessman's, stag's, stags'

22. run-on sentence

23. grandmother, washboard,

24. hen, feminine:
    chicks, indefinite;
    coop, neuter

25. <u>They</u> | <u>should have been wearing</u>

26. <u>(You)</u> | <u>remember</u>

27. declarative

28. statue

29. bad

30. confidently

LESSON 16   **Simple Prepositions**

Practice 16

a. *See book and preposition list*

b. *See book and preposition list*

c. *(Column 1)*
   aboard
   about
   above
   across
   after
   against
   along
   alongside
   amid
   among
   around
   at
   before
   behind
   below
   beneath
   (Column 2)

beside
besides
between
beyond
but
by
concerning
considering
despite
down
during
except
excepting
for
from
in
(Column 3)
inside
into
like
near
of
off
on
onto
opposite
out
outside
over
past
regarding
round
save
(Column 4)
since
through
throughout
till
to
toward
under
underneath
until
unto
up
upon
via

with
within
without

d. at, of, for

e. Like, without

f. In, of

g. below, of, from

h. Alongside, around

i. Beneath, at, into, despite, against, of

j. bibliomania

k. -mania

l. maniac

m. megalomania

More Practice 16

1. Before, of, in, with

2. Amid, at, without

3. to, on

4. to, with

5. Despite, of, from, of

6. With, around

7. inside, of

8. During, in, to, on

9. Before, at, with

10. After, without

Review Set 16

1. about, against, alongside, at, beneath

2. besides, beyond, considering, except, in

3. into, of, on, outside, over

4. throughout, to, underneath, up, within

5. into, in, in

6. sentence fragment

7. complete sentence

8. (is) flapping, flapped, (has) flapped

9. (a) have
   (b) are
   (c) does
   (d) am

10. (a) were
    (b) had
    (c) was
    (d) did

11. will interest

12. shall discuss

13. remains

14. enjoyed

15. tempos

16. shelves

17. bluffs

18. faxes

19. Walt Whitman, Quaker, Long Island, New York

20. produced

21. publishes

22. ambition, heresy, hypocrisy

23. brother, masculine;
    sister-in-law, feminine:
    beagle, indefinite;
    house, neuter;
    yard, neuter

24. Has (composed)

25. with, of

26. Walt Whitman | Has composed

27. interrogative

28. commendation

29. alluding

30. Alleys

Practice 17

a. *See book and preposition list*

b. *See book and preposition list*

c. (*Column 1*)
according to
across from
alongside of
along with
apart from
aside from
away from
because of
by means of
down from
except for
from among
from between
from under
in addition to
(*Column 2*)
in behalf of
in front of
in place of
in regard to
in spite of
inside of
next to
on account of
on behalf of
on top of
outside of
over to
owing to
prior to
round about

d. Because of

e. In addition to

f. by means of

g. prior to

h. According to

i. In spite of, down from, along with

j. megalo-

k. megalopolis

l. megalocardia

m. megalomania

More Practice 17

1. According to, to, alongside of

2. In addition to, on top of

3. except for

4. Aside from, in, in

5. in spite of

6. Round about, on, because of, of

7. to, in regard to, about

8. Along with, on, under, at

9. In front of, at, on behalf of, regarding, of

10. over to, behind

Review Set 17

1. to, for

2. according to

3. Because of

4. in front of, for, of

5. of, except

6. tortoise, concrete;
persistence, abstract;
perseverance, abstract;
discipline, abstract

7. Butch, concrete;
house, concrete;
back, concrete

8. could, have

9. (is) whizzing, whizzed, (has) whizzed

10. may, might, must

11. (a) is
(b) do
(c) have
(d) are

12. (a) did
    (b) was
    (c) did
    (d) were
13. eats
14. will celebrate
15. sentence fragment
16. . . . big meal. He searches . . . . (or) . . . big meal, and he . . . .
17. geese
18. moose
19. Langston Hughes, Harlem, New York, November, *The Weary Blues*
20. tortoise's, man's, siblings', sibling's
21. Keep in mind the finish line. (or) Keep the finish line in mind.
22. siblings, indefinite; tortoise, indefinite
23. tortoise | will triumph
24. tortoise | comes
25. plods
26. napped
27. hates
28. alley
29. Confidentially
30. elude

LESSON 18 The Perfect Tenses

Practice 18

a. have visited, present perfect
b. had migrated, past perfect
c. shall have completed, future perfect
d. cavalry
e. Calvary

More Practice 18

1. parrots | have adapted
2. Nancy | had adopted
3. lawmakers | will have waived
4. I | shall have finished
5. Uncle Bill | has arrived
6. you | Have seen

Review Set 18

1. In, with, because of
2. Across from, of
3. over to, on behalf of
4. will have learned, future perfect
5. Had wished, past perfect
6. has won, present perfect
7. will discover, future tense
8. had wandered, past perfect
9. has noticed, present perfect
10. trembles, present tense
11. (a) are
    (b) is
    (c) have
    (d) do
12. complete sentence
13. . . . to his mouth. The mouse . . . . (or) . . . to his mouth, but the mouse . . . .
14. (is) tickling, tickled, (has) tickled
15. has offered
16. amuses

17. will rescue

18. handfuls

19. tornadoes

20. wrenches

21. trays

22. On, Wasted, Yet, And

23. mouse | Will keep

24. mouse | could gnaw

25. mouse, concrete;
    fear, abstract;
    lion, concrete

26. lions', city's, mansion's

27. adapt

28. greatness

29. Hypocrisy

30. pleasant

LESSON 19 Verbals: The Gerund as a Subject

Practice 19

a. hunting

b. wine-making

c. Praying

d. Embalming

e. perfect tense

f. present tense

g. present tense

h. perfect tense

i. they're

j. their

k. there

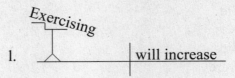

1. Exercising | will increase

More Practice 19

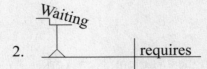

1. Waving | is

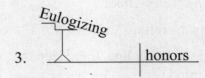

2. Waiting | requires

3. Eulogizing | honors

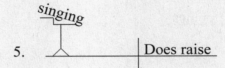

4. Sewing | is

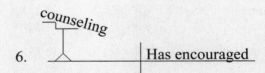

5. singing | Does raise

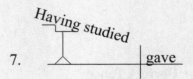

6. counseling | Has encouraged

7. Having studied | gave

Review Set 19

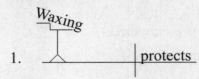

1. Waxing | protects

2. 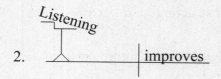 improves

3. Traitors | might expect

4. Diogenes | did speak

5. Having freed, present perfect tense

6. Gnawing, present tense

7. *See the preposition list in Lesson 17.*

8. (a) P
   (b) HV
   (c) P
   (d) HV
   (e) HV
   (f) P

9. On account of, in, by

10. has developed, present perfect tense

11. shall have read, future perfect tense

12. had partnered, past perfect tense

13. end, year, (club,) philosophies, life

14. (a) is
    (b) have
    (c) do
    (d) are

15. . . . encounter a lion. The fox . . . .

16. sentence fragment

17. (is) capturing, captured, (has) captured

18. has promised

19. succumbs

20. will have betrayed

21. tablespoonfuls

22. cargoes

23. clutches

24. donkeys

25. Langston Hughes, Lincoln University, Pennsylvania

26. betrayed

27. stomped

28. hypocrisy

29. homophones

30. Bibliomania

LESSON 20   **Capitalization: Titles, Outlines, Quotations**

Practice 20

a. I. Patriotic symbols
    A. American flag
    B. Eagle
  II. Patriotic songs
    A. "America"
    B. "God Bless America"

b. *Beauty and the Beast*

c. Concerning . . . , "Children . . . ."

d. C.S. Lewis commented, "They . . . ."

e. imminent

f. eminent

g. immanent

More Practice 20   *See Master Worksheets*

Review Set 20

1. *See preposition lists in Lessons 16 and 17.*

2. In, between, on behalf of

3. *Mrs. Frisbee and the Rats of N.I.M.H.*

4. *Otto of the Silver Hand*

5. I. Pearl S. Buck
    A. Nobel Prize . . .
    B. Bridge between . . .

6. When others . . . Pearl S. Buck did not . . . Nobel Prize . . . "Oh what a pity . . . Theodore Dreiser."

7. has remained, present perfect

8. had affected, past perfect

9. Writing

10. teaching

11. Having absorbed, perfect tense

12. Divorcing, present tense

13. chooses

14. have slapped

15. rallied

16. 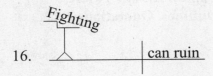 *Fighting* | can ruin

17. bat | will have ended

18. Never practice deceit.

19. (is) concluding, concluded, (has) concluded

20. scarves

21. shelves

22. banjos

23. mandolins

24. bat, concrete; nature, abstract

25. . . . win the battle. Then the bat . . . .

26. completed

27. imminent

28. their

29. mania

30. stature

LESSON 21   **The Progressive Verb Forms**

Practice 21

a. was learning, past progressive

b. shall be exercising, future progressive

c. is performing, present progressive

d. had been instructing, past perfect progressive

e. will have been seeing, future perfect progressive

f. has been howling, present perfect progressive

g. progressive

h. present

i. council

j. consul

k. counsel

l. Susan | had been lying

More Practice 21

1. Dominic | will have been working

2. Sophia | had been swimming

3. I | have been waiting

4. you | Have been watching

Review Set 21

1. In spite of, over, around

2. 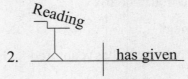 *Reading* | has given

3. . . . in their lives. They asked . . . .

4. "The Frogs Who Desired a King" is another of Aesop's fables.

5. Jupiter threw a log into the lake, saying, "There is your king."

6. outside

7. god, indefinite;
   queen, feminine;
   frogs, indefinite

8. army, frogs, Jupiter, time

9. (is) petitioning, petitioned, (has) petitioned

10. above, along, at

11. does

12. Have

13. Are

14. hoaxes

15. Nancys

16. will have provided, future perfect

17. were treating, past progressive

18. shall be learning, future progressive

19. is devouring, present progressive

20. will have been croaking, future perfect progressive

21. had been begging, past perfect progressive

22. Having received, perfect tense

23. Receiving, present tense

24. present

25. progressive

26. council

27. eminent

28. large

29. marches

30. had hopped

LESSON 22   Linking Verbs

Practice 22

a. is, am, are, was, were, be, being, been, look, feel, taste, smell, sound, seem, appear, grow, become, remain, stay

b. (*See Lesson 22*)

c. appears

d. no linking verb

e. seemed

f. remains

g. sounded

h. felt

i. no linking verb

j. smelled

k. aerobic

l. aphonic

m. anaerobic

n. phonic

o. without

More Practice 22

1. seemed

2. remains

3. appears

4. felt

5. remains

6. grew

7. stayed

8. smell

9. became

10. sounded

11. looks

12. are

13. were

14. taste

15. was

16. tastes, action

17. tastes, linking

18. sounds, action

19. sounds, linking

20. smelled, action

Review Set 22

1. is, am, are, was, were, be, being, been, look, feel, taste, smell, sound, seem, appear, grow, become, remain, stay

2. appears, linking

3. appears, action

4. tasted, action

5. is, linking

6. tasted, linking

7. sounded, action

8. Apart from, about

9. In addition to, for, of

10. Dr. H.R. Diogenes calls . . . Jerusalem cricket . . . .

11. complete sentence

12. run-on sentence

13. we | Will discover

14. (you) | do

15.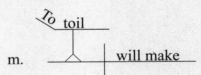
Giving | brings

16. declarative

17. weddings

18. syllabi

19. (is) hitching, hitched, (has) hitched

20. besides, but, down, excepting

21. (a) does
    (b) have
    (c) was

22. had comforted, past perfect

23. have experienced, present perfect

24. will have accomplished, future perfect

25. had been waiting

26. is underscoring

27. Having nursed, perfect tense

28. adopt

29. large

30. Imminent

LESSON 23   **The Infinitive as a Subject**

Practice 23

a. To discover

b. To weave

c. To have grown

d. perfect tense

e. present tense

f. lie

g. lay

h. lay

i. laid

j. lying

k. lay

l. laid

m. *To* toil | will make

More Practice 23

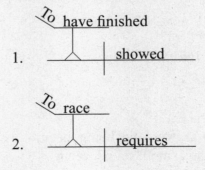

1. *To* have finished | showed

2. *To* race | requires

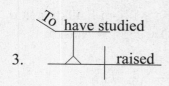

3. ___ raised

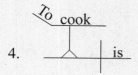

4. ___ is

To whisper

5. ___ might attract

To have quit

6. ___ would have signaled

Review Set 23

1. lay

2. gerund

3. infinitive

4. perfect

5. counsel

6. there

7. interrogative

8. fragment

9. princess, concrete;
   Prince, concrete;
   discouragement, abstract

10. matches

11. bedchambers

12. frays

13. nuclei

14. Willa Cather, Shenandoah Valley, Virginia, Nebraska

15. Her, *O Pioneers!*, I

16. I. Willa Cather
    A. Childhood
    B. Young adulthood

17. like, of, out, over

18. patches

19. (a) am
    (b) were
    (c) were

20. (is) preaching, preached, (has) preached

21. has tested, present perfect

22. is lying, present progressive tense

23. had been searching, past perfect progressive tense

24. (a) felt, action
    (b) felt, linking

25. Fishing, present tense

26. Having discovered, perfect tense

27. To have conceived, perfect tense

28. To prove, present tense

To have slept

29. ___ would have disqualified

Sleeping

30. ___ might have ruined

LESSON 24   Phrases and Clauses

Practice 24

a. clause

b. phrase

c. clause

d. phrase

e. Mt. McKinley | is located

f. trail | led

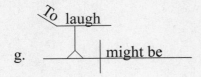

g.

h. sit

i. set

j. sat

k. set

More Practice 24

1. clause

2. phrase

3. clause

4. clause

5. phrase

6. phrase

7. clause

8. phrase

9. clause

10. phrase

Review Set 24

1. lie

2. imminent

3. proper

4. verbals

5. declarative

6. complete

7. king, concrete;
   guests, concrete;
   table, concrete;
   importance, abstract

8. avocados

9. caddies

10. elk

11. Concerning slavery, William Faulkner said, "To live . . . of A.D. 1955 . . . Alaska . . . ."

12. since, throughout, to, up, with

13. breathe

14. twirled

15. has

16. have

17. (is) diminishing, diminished, (has) diminished

18. had placed, past perfect

19. was planning, past progressive

20. After, in front of, along with

21. tasted, action

22. tasted, linking

23. To have chosen, perfect tense

24. Telling, present tense

25. 26. phrase

26. clause

27. clause

28. phrase

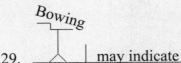

29.

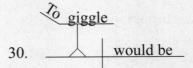

30.

LESSON 25

**The Direct Object •
Diagramming the Direct
Object**

Practice

a. gods

b. (none)

c. pyramids

d. food

e. 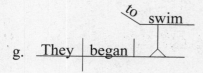 Egyptians | worshipped | gods

f. farmers | received | food

g. 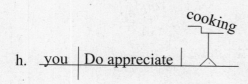 They | began | to swim

h. 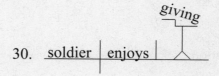 you | Do appreciate | cooking

i. perimeter

j. peri-

k. pericardium

l. periodontics

Review Set 25

1. cavalry

2. their

3. euphony

4. interrogative

5. run-on sentence

6. (pack,) dogs, (collection,) coins

7. axes

8. ploys

9. mice

10. cuffs

11. William Faulkner, New Albany, I

12. away from, by means of

13. clapped

14. will enter

15. does

16. (is) climbing, climbed, (has) climbed

17. will have married, future perfect

18. will be rescuing, future progressive

19. has been meeting, present perfect progressive

20. (a) feels, linking
    (b) feels, action

21. clause

22. phrase

23. Sharing, present tense

24. Having succeeded, perfect tense

25. To escape, present tense

26. To have fulfilled, perfect tense

27. (you) | rescue | princess

28. 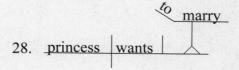 princess | wants | to marry

29. 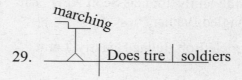 marching | Does tire | soldiers

30. soldier | enjoys | giving

LESSON 26   **Capitalization: People Titles, Family Words, School Subjects**

Practice 26

a. Spanish, French, Latin

b. Dad

c. Barbara Bush, President George H. W. Bush

d. My

e. mesomorph

f. ectomorph

g. morph

h. endomorph

More Practice 26   *See Master Worksheets*

Review Set 26

1. climate

2. statute

3. elude

4. declarative

5. sentence fragment

6. tree, concrete;
   impatience, abstract;
   discontentment, abstract

7. pasture, forest

8. piccolos

9. branches

10. Fitzgerald Family, Francis Scott Key, "The Star Spangled Banner"

11. Yes, I, Uncle Bob, Judge Hegarty, Latin, Greek

12. for, prior to, in

13. want

14. sounded, action

15. sounded, linking

16. clause

17. phrase

18. crushes

19. are cutting

20. had wished

21. tree

22. to rejoice

23. were listening, past progressive tense

24. had explained, past perfect

25. will be marrying, future progressive

26. 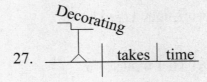 we | Shall decorate | tree

27. 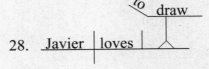 Decorating | takes | time

28. 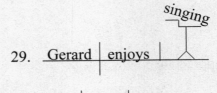 Javier | loves | to draw

29. Gerard | enjoys | singing

30. tree | wore | star

LESSON 27   **Descriptive Adjectives • Proper Adjectives**

Practice 27

a. sweaty, exhausted

b. ingenious, nervous

c. Irish, Scottish, Welsh

d. Columbus Day

Answers e-h may vary

e. Ex: enormous, yellow

f. Ex: sudden, awful

g. Ex: rug, custom

h. Ex: dress, egg

i. canon

j. cannon

k. cannon

More Practice 27   *See "Slapstick Story #2" in Master Worksheets*

Review Set 27

1. Heresy
2. There
3. sat
4. progressive
5. perfect
6. interrogative
7. run-on sentence
8. Tin Soldier, concrete; courage, abstract; loyalty, abstract; perseverance, abstract
9. lunches
10. Thursdays
11. attorneys-at-law
12. Dr. Bryce Darden, American Dental Association
13. Yesterday, I, Danish, Grandpa, "The Constant Tin Soldier"
14. should, would
15. plopped
16. has persevered, present perfect tense
17. will be playing, future progressive tense
18. has felt, action
19. has felt, linking
20. phrase
21. clause
22. Beneath, across from, with, in

23.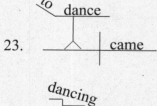

24.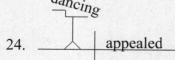

25.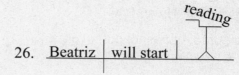

Bea | Has begun | to read

26. Beatriz | will start | reading

27. (you) | Honor | Tin Soldier

28. Faithful, valiant
29. mean, vicious, lonely, one-legged
30. graceful, compassionate

LESSON 28   The Limiting Adjectives • Diagramming Adjectives

Practice 28

a. telecommunication
b. tele-
c. telephone
d. telegraph
e. Aesop's, a, its
f. His, many
g. Several, these
h. That, some, this, a, few
i.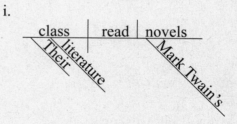

class | read | novels
Their | literature | Mark Twain's

More Practice 28   *See Master Worksheets*

Review Set 28

1. imperative
2. complete sentence
3. litter

4. (a) puffs
   (b) candies
   (c) cupfuls

5. The, I

6. My, Sir Lancelot, Have, I

7. of, off, on, onto, opposite, out, over, outside (*any four*)

8. From among, of

9. with

10. have

11. have

12. has

13. have behaved, present perfect tense

14. has been searching, present perfect progressive

15. was looking, linking

16. was looking, action

17. phrase

18. clause

19. To please, present tense

20. (is) reigning, reigned, (has) reigned

21. The, a, an, the

22. Some

23. continuing

24. sit

25. set

26. a-

27.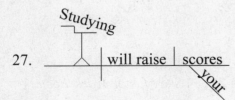

28.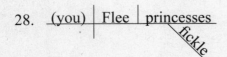

29.
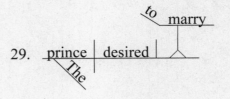

30.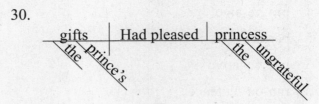

Practice 29

a. Many, South

b. The, Episcopal, God's

c. Celia's, Huntington Drive

d. Dear Father Tim,
   Thank you for your help.
   Gratefully,
   Cynthia

e. perspective

f. prospective

g. prospective

h. perspective

More Practice   *See Master Worksheets*

Review Set 29

1. perfect

2. lie

3. consul

4. without

5. interrogative

6. run-on sentence

7. People, concrete;
   discretion, abstract;
   palace, concrete

8. (a) studios
   (b) stimuli

9. Cary's, Greek, Hebrew, Latin

10. The, Smithsonian Institute

11. Hey, Grandpa, I

12. Does, East, West

13. Turn, Rosemead Boulevard, Greek

14. The, To, Regretfully, Mr. Babikian

15. According to, of, with, to

16. (a) were
    (b) am
    (c) are

17. had arranged, past perfect tense

18. had been singing, past perfect progressive tense

19. might smell, action

20. might smell, linking

21. clause

22. phrase

23. (is) answering, answered, (has) answered

24. the, many, the, one, the, magnificent, the, little

25. That, the, king's, its, proper, the, royal

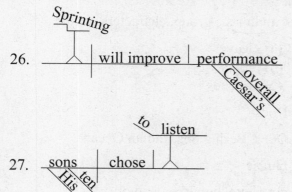

26.

27.

28. was listening

29. has created

30. shall write

LESSON 30   No Capital Letter

Practice 30

a. proponent

b. project

c. pro-

d. program

e. Mother-in-law Joyce

f. no capital letters

g. Spanish, Greek, California

h. Beau, Belle

i. California, Chinese, Australian

More Practice 30   *See Master Worksheets*

Review Set 30

1. exclamatory

2. sentence fragment

3. nightingale, concrete;
   emperor, concrete;
   pleasure, abstract

4. fisherman, opinion, bird

5. (a) children
   (b) sketches
   (c) Larrys

6. Yesterday, Uncle Eric, Meet, Huntington Beach, Wednesday, Chinese

7. Because of, at, of

8. hopped

9. is harmonizing

10. (a) does
    (b) do
    (c) did

11. shall have earned, future perfect tense

12. will have been singing, future perfect progressive tense

13. appears, action

14. appears, linking

15. clause

16. phrase

17. (is) smiling, smiled, (has) smiled

18. The, arrogant, pedantic, his, jewel-studded

19. any, that real

20. German ruler, Japanese assembly

21. American youth

22. Having pleased, perfect tense

23. completed

24. city

25. cavalry

26. Their

27.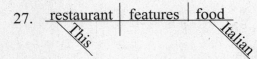

28.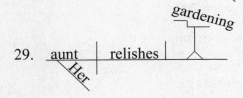

29.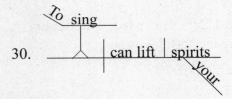

30.

LESSON 31   Transitive and Intransitive Verbs

Practice 31

a. <u>fulfills</u>, *demands, transitive

b. <u>glows</u>, no direct object, intransitive

c. <u>procures</u>, *princess, transitive

d. <u>is slain</u>, no direct object, intransitive

e. ante-

f. antedate

g. antebellum

h. anteroom

More Practice 31

1. transitive, lamp

2. intransitive

3. intransitive

4. intransitive

5. transitive, gates

6. transitive, feast

7. intransitive

8. intransitive

9. transitive, lamp

10. intransitive

Review Set 31

1. exclamatory

2. run-on sentence

3. girl, feminine;
   lady, feminine;
   husband, masculine;
   dog, indefinite

4. (author's) group, characters, whale

5. (a) leaves
   (b) reefs
   (c) finches

6. Does

7. Does, Bering Sea, Indian Ocean

8. phrase

9. am, were, being, must, will

10. through, throughout, till, to, toward

11. on top of, of, to

12. seems, linking

13. is looking, linking

14. will be blowing, action

15. were watching

16. fizzes

17. (a) have
    (b) have
    (c) has

18. block, (is) blocking, blocked, (has) blocked

19. enormous, grouchy

20. The, a, an

21. Alsatian dog

22. Having settled, perfect tense

23.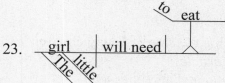

24.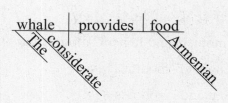

25. continuing

26. present

27. present

28. adapt

29. straighten

30. counsel

LESSON 32 — Object of the Preposition • The Prepositional Phrase

Practice 32

a. In a *group;
   of *words;
   with the same *letter or *sound

b. According to this *definition;
   through *thick and *thin;
   of *alliteration

c. in *poetry, *prose, and *oratory

d. from *beginning;
   to *end

e. forcible

f. forceful

g. forceful

More Practice 32

1. of *land;
   between the *Mediterranean Sea and the *Jordan River

2. In spite of its small *size;
   of the ancient *world

3. over *Israel;
   from the world's two oldest *cultures

4. through *Israel;
   to their *battles

5. Because of its *location;
   by *enemies

6. along Israel's *coast

7. to the *sea;
   from *it

8. Across from the *Sea of Galilee;
   on the *map;
   of *Nazareth

9. According to *historians;
   in *Nazareth;
   during his *childhood

10. through the *middle;
    of the deepest *fault;
    in the *world

11. beyond *Israel;
    into the *continent;
    of *Africa

12. below sea *level

Review Set 32

1. declarative

2. complete sentence

3. completed

4. have

5. intransitive

6. transitive

7. eminent

8. without

9. lie

10. wanderlust

11. spots

12. (a) barracudas or barracuda
    (b) contraltos
    (c) trenches

13. Yes, I, Aunt Della, My, San Diego, Tuesday

14. In "The Story of the Four Little Children Who Went Around the World," Violet

15. clause

16. before, behind, below, beneath, beside, besides, between, beyond, but, by

17. Prior to, with, on, by, with

18. may, might, must

19. look, feel, taste, sound, smell

20. pried

21. demolish, (is) demolishing, demolished, (has) demolished

22. remain, linking

23. remains, linking

24. has bitten, transitive

25. are continuing, intransitive

26. These, curious, eventful, foreign

27.

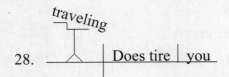

28.

29.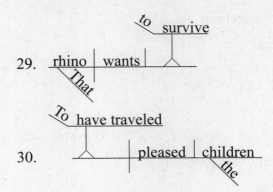

30.

LESSON 33 **The Prepositional Phrase as an Adjective • Diagramming**

Practice 33

a. "concerning the care of young children" modifies *articles*;
   "of Christianity" modifies *truth*

b. "in her field" modifies *expert*

c. "for mothers and fathers" modifies *tips*

d. "of England" modifies *queen*

e. "to England" modifies *trip*;
   "of mine" modifies *dream*

f. "in London" modifies *people*

g.

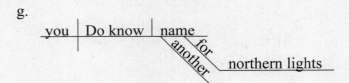

h.

i. hydrophobia

j. -phobia

k. agoraphobia

l. claustrophobia

Review Set 33

1. exclamatory

2. sentence fragment

3. (crowd,) competition, king

4. kings', crown's, James's

5. (a) servicemen
   (b) torpedoes
   (c) wrenches

6. A, Twenty-one

7. Lord Calomel, Pacific Ocean, Gulf of California

8. phrase

9. by means of, between, of

10. In addition to *tests;
    of physical *strength;
    of *intelligence

11. Prior to the math *problem;
    of the *kings

12. Owing to a *tie;
    between first and second *place;
    of *kingship;
    on two *legs

13. has discovered, present perfect tense

14. shall be reading, future progressive tense

15. Competing, present tense

16. To have beaten, perfect tense

17. sounded, action

18. sounded, linking

19. has revealed, transitive

20. have been transformed, intransitive

21. The, forgetful, the, resourceful, the, missing

22. Nine, one

23. Tudor castle

24. lay

25. laid

26. peri-

27. around

28. morph

29.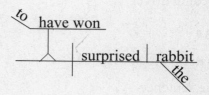

30.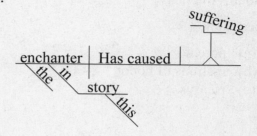

LESSON 34   **The Indirect Object**

Practice 34

a. discreet

b. homophones

c. discrete

d. discreet

e. me

f. no indirect object

g. us

h. the government

i. Fido brought newspaper / me / the

j. Dad made sandwiches / us

More Practice 34

1. me

2. him

3. us

4. none

5. them

6. Mr. Habib

7. that speeding driver

Review Set 34

1. interrogative

2. complete sentence

3. South America

4. beanstalk

5. (a) porches
   (b) matrons of honor
   (c) Henrys

6. In

7. Shall, I, "The Pumpkin Giant," Monday

8. clause

9. me

10. In front of, of

11. Round about the *country;
    of the *castle;
    with the *courtyard;
    in *children

12. has, have, had

13. (a) were
    (b) were
    (c) were

14. will have been circulating, future perfect progressive

15. has provided, present perfect tense

16. has offered, action

17. is feeling, linking

18. has been throwing, transitive

19. will perish, intransitive

20. scattered, smashed, little, yellow, long, green

21. his

22. Pumpkin Giant's castle

23. form

24. they're

25. large

26.

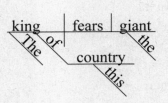

27.

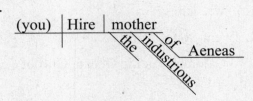

28.

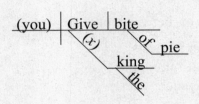

29.

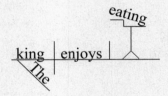

30.

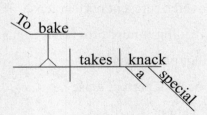

LESSON 35   **The Period • Abbreviations**

Practice 35

a. I. Berlin Wall
      A. Constructed in 1961
      B. Dismantled in 1989

b. East Germany constructed the Berlin Wall in 1961 to keep East Germans from escaping to West Germany.

c. Study the reasons for escaping.

d. P.T. Barnum was a famous American showman.

e. V.I.P. is the abbreviation for "very important person."

f. Taggart's curfew was 11:00 p.m.

g. Dr. Chin is over six feet tall.

h. Mrs. Goody's recipe calls for two teaspoons of baking powder.

i. The staff meets the third Tuesday of each month to discuss upcoming school events.

j. Venezuela occupies the northeast portion of the South American continent.

k. Eduardo Perez, Ph.D., described the location of Mount Everest.

l. (a) Fri.
   (b) Jan.
   (c) Dr.
   (d) Ave.

m. synchronize

n. syn-

o. syndicate

p. synonym

Review Set 35

1. declarative

2. run-on sentence

3. was winking, past progressive

4. had been complaining, past perfect progressive

5. citizens, Rootabaga Country, (Judaism)

6. mother, feminine;
   children, indefinite

7. (a) earfuls
   (b) ways
   (c) watches

8. The, Alaskan

9. In, "The Pumpkin Giant," Mary E. Wilkins, He's

10. phrase

11. Next to the *country;
    of *Balloon Pickers

12. of the *train;
    on account of a *cow;
    on the *tracks

13. Last August, Dr. Snipe moved into a home on Azusa Street.

14. can, could

15. (a) does
    (b) do
    (c) do

16. tasted, action

17. tasted, linking

18. are wearing, transitive

19. is chugging, intransitive

20. conductor

21. you

22. Some

23.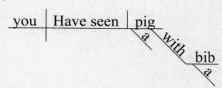

We | will ride | train
the

24.

you | Have seen | pig
a with
bib
a

25.

Clowns | presented | show
(x) us   a of somersaults

26.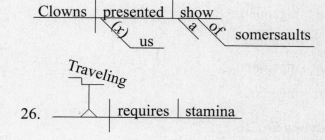

Traveling

requires | stamina

27.

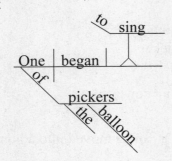

28. Eminent

29. lay

30. around

LESSON 36   Coordinating Conjunctions

Practice 36

a. and
   or
   for
   so

b. but, nor, yet

c. and, but, or, nor, for, yet, so

d. and

e. but

f. yet

g. but, for, and

i. or

j. so, and

k. ingenuous

l. ingenuous

m. ingenious

n. ingenious

Review Set 36

1. Mrs. Conseco will meet you on Friday at three p.m.

2. At birth, Robert A. Hake weighed nine pounds, two ounces.

3. and, but, or, for, nor, yet, so

4. and, but, for, yet

5. complete sentence

6. may save, transitive

7. (a) mice
   (b) lice
   (c) turkeys

8. We, Lake Mary, Sierra Nevada Mountains

9. Did, Uncle Herbert, "Prince Rabbit"

10. Sometimes, Northeast, Southwest

11. Across from Brer Fox's *fire

12. study, (is) studying, studied, (has) studied

13. had assumed, past perfect

14. has been making, present perfect progressive

15. That, one, smart

16. period

17. period

18. period

19. period

20. periods

21. gerund

22. present

23.

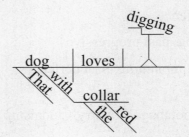

24.

She | gave | bath
(x) dog
her

25. phrase

26. clause

27. infinitive

28. form

29. canon

30. distant

LESSON 37

Compound Subjects and Predicates • Diagramming Compounds

Practice 37

a. orthography

b. graphy

c. biography

d. photography

e. choreography

f.
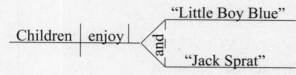

g.
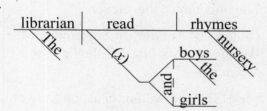

h.
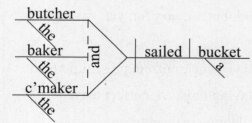

i.
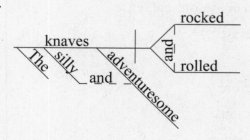

Review Set 37

1. long

2. perspective

3. before

4. Antebellum

5. forceful

6. transitive

7. clause

8. had tasted, action

9. sentence fragment

10. sloth

11. rabbit, indefinite; well, neuter

12. (a) elk
    (b) brothers-in-law
    (c) boxes

13. The House of Representatives, Senate, President of the United States

14. A, Uncle Remus, Wasn't

15. concerning, considering

16. away from the *others

17. "of this contest" modifies "victor"

18. shall have learned, future perfect tense

19. had been running, past progressive

20. will discover

21. convinces

22. Mr. Remus reports that the ten-pound fox sinks into the well, lifting the two-pound rabbit to the surface

23. Harry P. Broomhead, Jr, has worked for the Western Codliver Co. since January of 1955.

24. I.Uncle Remus's stories
    A. "Briar Patch"
    B. "Down the Well"
    C. "Dinner with Brer Rabbit"

25. and, but, or, for, nor, yet, so
26. or

27.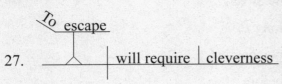

28.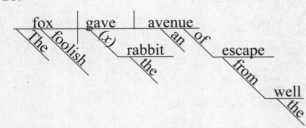

29.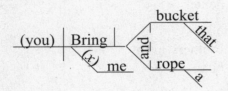

30.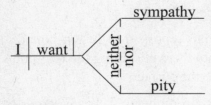

LESSON 38   **Correlative Conjunctions**

Practice 38

a. either—or

b. Neither—nor

c. Both—and

d. Not only—but also

e.

```
       sympathy
I | want \ neither
          nor
       pity
```

f. dissension

g. audacity

h. treason

1. imperative

2. Last, May, I, *The Lion, Witch, Wardrobe*, C.S. Lewis

3. pessimism

4. (a) ladies
   (b) men
   (c) handfuls

5. aboard, about, above, across, after, against, along, alongside

6. in spite of the rabbit's *boasting

7. (a) was
   (b) were
   (c) were

8. Does smell, action

9. smells, linking

10. has been hopping, intransitive

12. Can trap, transitive

13. The, ingenious, the, clever

14. On the first Tuesday in September, Ms. Weezle . . . Fox Place in the Frazier Mountains.

15. Mr. Hoogle drove northeast on Canyon Boulevard to see Dr. Rudy P. Cruz.

16. and, but, or, nor, for, yet, so

17. or

18. Have synchronized, present perfect

19. Having finished, perfect tense

20. laughing, present tense

21. To boast, present tense

22. phrase

23. fear

24. before

25. forcible

26. together

27. ingenuous

28.
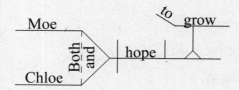

29.
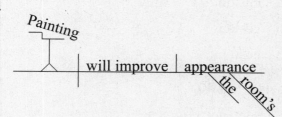

30.
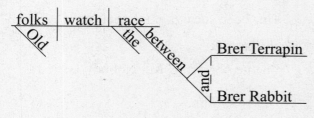

h.
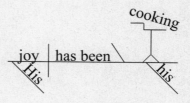

i. He | became \ expert
             \ an

Review Set 39

1. exclamatory

2. Mr. Webster, ouphe, word, goblin, elf

3. (a) hankies
   (b) keys
   (c) pitches

4. Benito, Hey, Grandpa

5. Goldie Mae Sharp

6. tap, (is) tapping, tapped, (has) tapped

7. clause

8. Outside of the *house;
   on the *door

9. invited, transitive

10. (a) Have
    (b) Does

11. was waiting, past progressive tense

12. her, old, weak, some, crispy, brown, seasoned

13. I. Ouphes
        A. Rich
        B. Hermits
        C. Disguised as old men

14. Please meet me on Huntington Drive at two p.m. this Tuesday.

15. Mr. and Mrs. Salazar have been happily married since August.

16. and, but, or, nor, for, yet, so

17. or

LESSON 39   **Diagramming Predicate Nominatives**

Practice 39

a. root

b. Greek (or Latin)

c. chronometer

d. chronology

e. chronobiology

f.
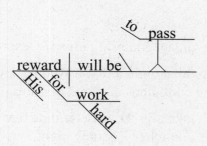

g. King James | was \ monarch
                    \ a

18. neither/nor;
    not only/but also;
    either/or;
    both/and

19. Neither/nor

20. not only/but also

21. seemed, linking

22. Having dreamed, perfect tense

23. To think, present tense

24. fear

25. discrete

26. synonyms

27. ingenuous

28. peri-

29.
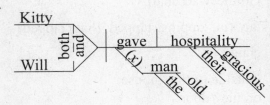

30.
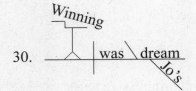

LESSON 40   **Noun Case**

Practice 40

a. nominative case, subject

b. nominative case, predicate nominative

c. possessive case

d. nominative case, subject

e. nominative case, predicate nominative

f. O.P.

g. I.O.

h. D.O.

i. nominative case

j. objective case

k. possessive case

l. objective case

m. costume

n. custom

o. custom

p. costume

Review Set 40

1. sentence fragment

2. phrase

3. Has been sneaking, intransitive

4. declarative

5. (name,) brownie, Mr. Nobody

6. (a) calves
   (b) roofs
   (c) children

7. felt, linking

8. At, American, French, Spanish, Latin

9. In, Southwest

10. jog, (is) jogging, jogged, (has) jogged

11. Apart from his *appearance;
    in the whole *world

12. squelches

13. were hissing

14. had trapped

15. The, old, an, adequate, a, famished, each

16. Upon arrival at eight a.m. on Wednesday,
    the young cook finds . . . food missing

17. It doesn't take a Ph.D. to determine that a
    brownie . . . kitchen Tuesday night.

18. Neither/nor

19. both/and

20. To have frustrated, perfect tense

21. teasing, present tense

22. set

23. lie

24. structure

25. perspective

26. before

27. objective case

28.
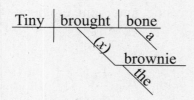

29.
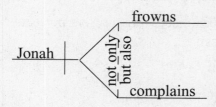

30.
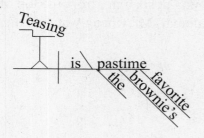

LESSON 41   **Diagramming Predicate Adjectives**

Practice 41

a.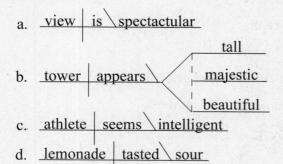

b.

c.

d.

e. hyper-

f. hyperactivity

g. hyperglycemia

h. hyperbole

Review Set 41

1. try/tries, (is) trying, tried, (has) tried

2. has remained, action

3. phrase

4. imperative

5. run-on

6. (a) bibliographies
   (b) justices of the peace
   (c) wives

7. The, President, United States, George MacDonald's, "The Light Princess"

8. "with no children" modifies "king"

9. were chatting

10. was

11. has delivered, present perfect tense

12. has been learning, present perfect progressive tense

13. was christened, intransitive

14. had forgotten, transitive

15. Sour, spiteful, many, peevish, contemptuous, her

16. I. Daughters of the American Revolution
    A. Mrs. Adeline Curtis's comments
    B. Research by Miss Virginia Otto, Ph.D.

17. and, but, or, for, nor, yet, so

18. fairy

19. victim

20. predicate

21. subject

22. Immanent

23. eminent

24. aphonic

25. set

26. lay

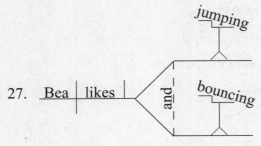

27. Bea | likes ... jumping and bouncing

28. aunt | became \ treacherous / Her

29. you | Have experienced | loss / the of gravity

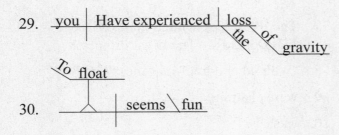

30. To float | seems \ fun

LESSON 42   **Comparison Adjectives**

Practice 42

a. healthier, comparative

b. trimmest, superlative

c. older, comparative

d. most fabulous, superlative

e. riper, comparative

f. more, comparative

g. wider, widest

h. more generous, most generous

i. hypo-

j. Hypocalcemia

k. Hypothyroidism

l. hypoglycemia

Review Set 42

1. objective case

2. trim, (is) trimming, trimmed, (has) trimmed

3. interrogative

4. clause

5. have remained, linking

6. will volunteer, transitive

7. (a) bunches
   (b) tablespoonfuls
   (c) Debbys

8. On, Monday, Quan, James, Chinese

9. treason, climactic, anteroom, eminent, fewer

10. were

11. have

12. has troubled, present perfect

13. have been discussing, present perfect progressive

14. solution

15. king, queen

16. This morning at six a.m., from the top of Mount Palomar, Mr. Chang watched the sun rise.

17. solution

18. tyrannical

19. nominative

20. case

21. nominative

22. fear

23. discreet

24. graphy

25. Dissension

26. Having tried, perfect tense

27. to swim, present tense

28. tear | might be \ solution / A human a

29. Water | will offer | freedom / (x) from / princess the little weightlessness her

30.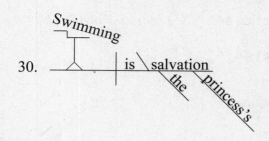

LESSON 43 — Irregular Comparison Adjectives

Practice 43

a. much
b. many
c. best
d. more
e. little
f. better
g. luxuriant
h. luxurious
i. luxurious
j. luxuriant

More Practice 43

1. less
2. better
3. worst
4. better
5. more reliable
6. more
7. most conniving
8. smarter
9. farther
10. fewer
11. fewer
12. less

1. run-on sentence
2. phrase
3. (a) stripes
   (b) cliffs
   (c) ponies
4. Christina, Heidelberg, Germany
5. Amid *fanfare and *applause; down from the *platform; among the *people
6. Did rescue, transitive
7. Does seem, linking
8. has made, present perfect tense
9. will have been swimming, future perfect progressive
10. shall have discussed, future perfect
11. princess
12. (An) exasperated, (the) difficult, (a)
13. rescue/rescues, (is) rescuing, rescued, (has) rescued
14. objective case
15. Thursday morning, Dr. Cabrera took giant steps to avoid the cracks in the sidewalk on West Hope Street.
16. home
17. indirect object
18. direct object
19. object of a preposition
20.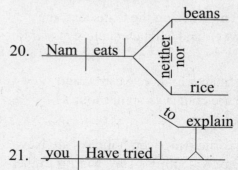
21.
22. Having ruined, perfect tense
23. to empty, present tense

24. sillier, silliest

25. larger

26. audacity

27. chrono

28. adapt

29. cacophony

30. fear

LESSON 44 The Comma, Part 1: Dates, Addresses, Series

Practice 44

a. hetero-

b. heterogeneous

c. heteronyms

d. heterophony

e. The Emancipation Proclamation of January 1, 1863, was issued by President Abraham Lincoln.

f. On March 13, 1862, President Lincoln forbade the Union army officers to return fugitive slaves.

g. Christmas fell on Tuesday, December 25, in the year 2001.

h. The Statue of Liberty is located on Liberty Island, New York, New York 10004.

i. San José, Costa Rica, attracts many tourists each year.

j. Will you visit Madrid, Spain, this spring?

k. We will enjoy seeing the Coliseum, the Eiffel Tower, and Michelangelo's *David* in Europe.

l. Italy, Germany, France, Austria, and England are countries on our tour's itinerary.

m. Some favorite American holidays are New Year's Day, Valentine's Day, Martin Luther King Day, President's Day, St. Patrick's Day, and Independence Day.

More Practice 44   *See Master Worksheets*

Review Set 44

1. fewer

2. abstract

3. taller

4. many

5. human

6. elude

7. Prospective

8. Ingenious

9. subject

10. linking

11. Miss Vong glanced up at the San Gabriel Mountains as she hurried to her nine a.m. interview at the Varoom Appliance Co.

12. (a) deer
    (b) videos
    (c) matches

13. The, If

14. Please, Father

15. on the *bus;
    underneath the *seat;
    with the *rest;
    of her *stuff

16. hisses

17. is offering

18. the, the, prince's, brave

19. His, many

20. agreeable

21. has been lying, intransitive

22. sneeze, (is) sneezing, sneezed, (has) sneezed

23. nominative case

24. phrase

25. clause

26. sentence fragment

27.

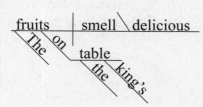

28.

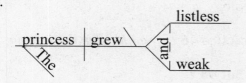

29.

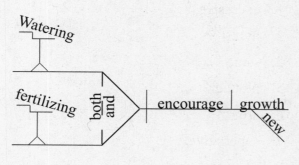

30.

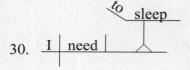

LESSON 45   **Appositives**

Practice 45

a. epic

b. epoch

c. epoch

d. Epic

e. Benjamin Franklin

f. the Franklin stove

g. Ben Franklin (inventor) made lightning rod

h. Ex: The American Philosophical Society, a discussion group, was organized by Benjamin Franklin.

i. Ben Franklin signed the Declaration of Independence, a document that declares . . . .

More Practice 45   *See "Slapstick Story #3" in Master Worksheets*

Review Set 45

1. might waive, transitive

2. team, mascot, game

3. team's, teams', mascot's

4. complete sentence

5. (a) radii or radiuses
   (b) torpedoes
   (c) crutches

6. Aunt Clara, Uncle Meredith, "The Little Princess."

7. Let's wash the dishes, fold the laundry, and mow the lawn.

8. appears, linking

9. was drowning

10. saves

11. From under the *water; of the *prince; from the *snare

12. the, gallant, her, first

13. linking

14. comparative

15. biggest

16. greater

17. On the first Monday in August, Mr. Moses A. Zamora will be here at two p.m. to discuss the benefits of Healthquest, Inc.

18. either/or,
    both/and,
    not only/but also,
    neither/nor

19. bride

20. nominative case

21. objective case

22.

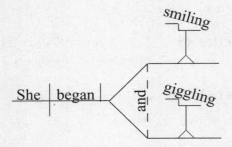

23.

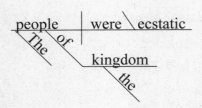

24. phrase

25. To have punished, perfect

26. costume

27. excessive

28. sincere

29. smiled

30. were

LESSON 46

The Comma, Part 2: Direct Address, Appositives, Academic Degrees

Practice 46

a. Students, Robert Fulton began his career as an American painter

b. Did you know, Raffi, that Robert Fulton invented machines for cutting marble, for spinning flax, and for twisting hemp into rope?

c. *Fulton the First*, the first steam-propelled warship, was developed by Robert Fulton.

d. Jack London, author of *To Build a Fire*, battled the elements of nature in many of his stories.

e. Sara Brown, D.V.M., informed us that our dog needed to lose weight.

f. Polly Wafer, R.N., collapsed into bed after working a twelve-hour shift at the hospital.

g. theo-

h. theocrat

i. theologian

j. theology

More Practice 46 *See Master Worksheets*

Review Set 46

1. excessive

2. hypo-

3. same

5. plotted

6. are

7. superlative

8. comparative

9. positive

10. sentence fragment

11. clause

12. Princess Zena, Bobo, mother

13. (a) stitches
    (b) simpletons
    (c) portfolios

14. The, Shall, Bobo

15. at the *castle;
    on ridiculous *errands

16. Outside of *Tilda;
    in the *community

17. have sent, present perfect tense

18. will be searching, intransitive

19. Does remain, linking

20. (a) slower, slowest
    (b) more, most enthusiastic
    (c) subtler, subtlest

21. drop, (is) dropping, dropped, (has) dropped

22. Bobo relies on Tilda, the kitchen maid.

23. and, but, or, for, nor, yet, so

24. H. Bestron wrote a story about the Kingdom of the East and the Kingdom of the West.

25. nominative case

26. Having received, perfect

27. My mother, Isabel Curtis, works at a library in Arcadia, California.

28.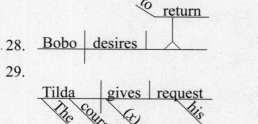

29.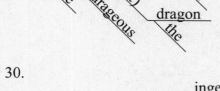

30.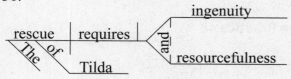

LESSON 47   **Overused Adjectives • Unnecessary Articles**

Practice 47

Answers will vary.

a. error-filled, boring, depressing

b. healthy, happy, beautiful, lovely

c. pleasant, exciting, enjoyable

d. moldy, dry, old, stale

e. That sort of assignment is difficult for most people.

f. Harriet brought both of them to the wedding.

g. anecdote

h. antidote

i. antidote

j. anecdote

Review Set 47

1. fewer

2. Human

3. waves

4. syn-

5. custom

6. phrase

7. lives, intransitive

8. John, ⟨frustration⟩ fairies, forest

9. (a) tomatoes
   (b) fairies
   (c) ladies-in-waiting

10. I. "The Dutch Cheese"
    A. Results of obstinacy
    B. Effects of a loving nature

11. Inside the *forest;
    with mischievous *ideas

12. run-on sentence

13. (a) has
    (b) have
    (c) Have

14. have been harassing, present perfect progressive tense

15. have fled, present perfect tense

16. must have felt, linking

17. The, mischievous, the

18. one, great, round, an, impish

19. both/and,
    either/or,
    neither/nor,
    not only/but also

20. the

21. On Tuesday, January 14, 2002, Clifton Junior High School presented Mr. De La Mare's "The Dutch Cheese" as a play.

22. Please send all mail to 80 Easing Way, Oghh City, Fairyland.

23. nominative case

24. objective case

25. Armando, a college student, plays the piano, guitar, and bass.

26.

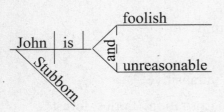

27.

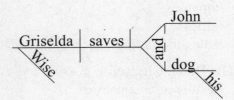

28.

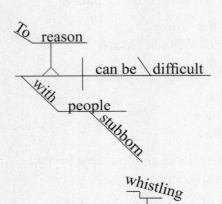

29.

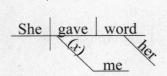

30.

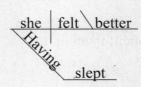

LESSON 48
Verbals as Adjectives: Infinitives and Participles

Practice 48

a. historic

b. historic

c. historical

d. historical

e. to flee; noun

f. to do, adjective that modifies "tasks"

g. Having followed, runner, perfect tense

h. leaping, teenager, present tense

i. frightened, animal, past tense

j.

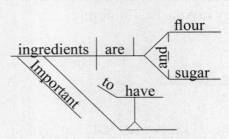

k.

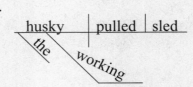

More Practice 48

1.

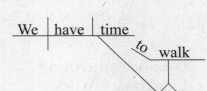

2.

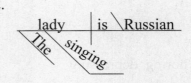

3.

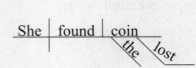

4.

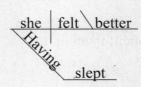

5.

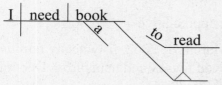

6.

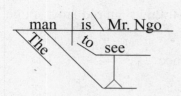

Review Set 48

1. exclamatory

2. intransitive

3. appositive

4. custom

5. exaggeration

6. epoch

7. theo-

8. taller

9. People . . . enjoy storytelling. A grandmother . . . .

10. (a) Saturdays
    (b) theologies
    (c) calves

11. lived, intransitive

12. A, Tale, Three, Tails, I, Charles J. Finger

13. clause

14. Next to the old *lady, with the *cigar, between her *teeth

15. with long sweeping *hairs, like a *horse

16. (a) were
    (b) was
    (c) were

17. Does smell, action

18. had been clearing, past perfect progressive

19. dwindle(s), (is) dwindling, dwindled, (has) dwindled

20. French

21. wise, old, caring

22. both/and

23. On Saturday, June 2, Mrs. Vong will inspect the plumbing, roofing, and painting on the house at 87 Thicket Road, Jungle City, Africa.

24. wizard, owl

25. possessive case

26. an angry wizard

27.

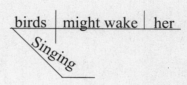

28.

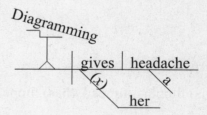

29.

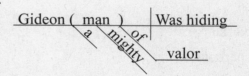

30.

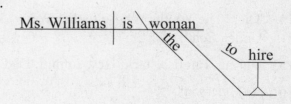

LESSON 49   **Pronouns and Antecedents**

Practice 49

a. he/Cory;
   it/novel

b. he/Dirk

c. he/Hanfu

d. they/boots

e. While Georgiana and Marissa were shopping, Marissa bought a new suede jacket.

f. The jacket cost five hundred dollars.

g. philanthropist

h. philologist

i. philatelist

j. phil-

Review Set 49

1. transitive

2. demonstrative

3. possessive

4. epoch

5. god

6. luxuriant

7. hyperbole

8. recording

9. under

10. mystifies

11. shall learn

12. flip(s), (is) flipping, flipped, (has) flipped

13. twins, hare, (moonlight)

14. The, "The Youths Whose Father Was Under, Sea"

15. During, English, Jack, Hey, John, I, Dad

16. (a) persons
    (b) safes
    (c) foxes

17. phrase

18. of *provisions;
    with the red *fox;
    along with the fox's *wife and *children

19. will have searched, future perfect tense

20. smoother

21. most appreciative

22. On March 31, 2002, fifty needy families received five-pound hams from Deborah Schneider, Ph.D.

23. The Hag of Hollows, an old lady, spoke with John.

24. run-on sentence

25. objective case

26. Does smell, linking

27. Mr. Angles, a plumber, fixed our leaky faucet.

28. a

29.

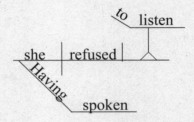

30.

LESSON 50 — **The Comma, Part 3: Greetings and Closings, Last Name First, Introductory and Interrupting Elements, Afterthoughts, Clarity**

Practice 50

a. Dear Alana,
   Have you heard the expression "The handwriting is on the wall?" What does it mean?
   Love,
   Clara

b. Use the card catalog to find the writings of "Jefferson, Thomas."

c. "The handwriting is on the wall," I believe, refers to an imminent occurrence

d. The Hippocratic Oath, they say, is taken by all physicians before they begin practicing medicine.

e. No, I am not familiar with the words in the Hippocratic Oath.

f. It includes the duties and responsibilities of the physician, I think.

g. With Molly, Curtis acts silly.

h. Ever since, she has eaten more nutritious foods.

i. protagonist

j. antagonist

j. foreshadowing

l. melodrama

More Practice 50   *See Master Worksheets*

Review Set 50

1. least

2. Do

3. humane

4. passion

5. megalomania

6. their

7. anecdote

8. complete sentence

9. In Cuautla, Mexico, so the story goes, duendes let out chickens, tease dogs, and turn on lights.

10. On behalf of *Lorenzo; about hard *work

11. No, other, her, little, torn

12. spies, transitive

13. Is crying, intransitive

14. and, but, or, for, nor, yet, so

15. Neither/nor

16. nominative case

17. objective case

18. Mr. B. Smart, our new principal, arrived on Tuesday, September 3, 2002.

19. Lorenzo's mother

20. try (or tries), (is) trying, tried, (has) tried

21. phrase

22. washes

23. has learned

24. (a) indices
     (b) pennies
     (c) knives

25. lower, lowest

26. She surprises both of them with a clean house.

27. she/Sarita;
    her/Sarita

28. are showing, present progressive

29.

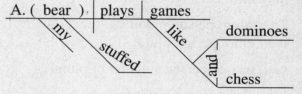

30.

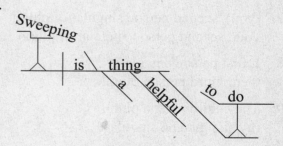

LESSON 51   **Personal Pronouns**

Practice 51

a. polygon

b. -gon

c. octagon

d. pentagon

e. heptagon

f. hexagon

g. me, first person

h. she, third person

i. you, second person

j. us, plural

k. me, singular

l. indirect object

m. direct object

n. possession

o. subject

More Practice 51

1. we, first person plural;
   you, second person singular or plural

2. they, third person plural

3. (you), second person singular or plural;
   him, third person singular

4. They, third person plural;
   their, third person plural

5. you, second person singular or plural

6. her, third person singular

7. (you), second person singular or plural;
   your, second person singular or plural

8. I, first person singular;
   them, third person plural

9. They, third person plural;
   my, first person singular

10. She, third person singular;
    us, first person plural

11. we, subject;
    you, object

12. they, subject

13. you, subject;
    him, object

14. they, subject;
    their, possessive

15. you, subject

16. her, object

17. you, subject;
    your, possessive

18. I, subject;
    them, object

19. they, subject;
    my, possessive

20. she, subject
    us, object

Review set 51

1. sentence fragment

2. clause

3. is guarding, transitive

4. (a) appears, linking
   (b) appears, action

5. (a) candies
   (b) beaches
   (c) skies

6. interrogative

7. In, China, Mustapha

8. I. "Aladdin"
   A. Childhood
   B. African magician
   C. Genies

9. Except for his *mother;
   of Aladdin's *lamp and *ring

10. grin(s), (is) grinning, grinned, (has)
    granned

11. The, African, a, large, Chinese

12. Examples: rude, cruel, unkind, hateful

13. Yes, the genie provided Aladdin and his
    mother with food, clothing, and riches

14. neither, nor

15. Mustapha

16. Ex. The sorcerer arrived from his native country, Africa.

17. pronoun

18. antecedent

19. before

20. go

21. before

22. she, Jenny;
    her, Jenny;
    her, Jenny;
    her, Jenny

23. religion

24. anecdotes

25. historic

26. loving

27.

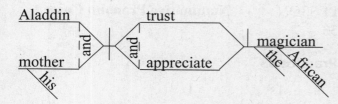

28.

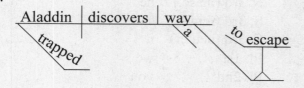

29.

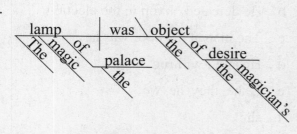

30.

Practice 52

   a. allegory

   b. caricature

   c. cliché

   d. denouement

   e. stolen

   f. blown

   g. tore

   h. frozen

   i. bore

   j. broke

   k. thrown

   l. worn

   m. swore

   n. rang

   o. sang

   p. drunk

More Practice 52

1. blew, blown

2. knew, known

3. threw, thrown

4. grew, grown

5. bore, borne

6. tore, torn

7. wore, worn

8. swore, sworn

9. began, begun

10. rang, rung

11. sang, sung

12. drank, drunk

13. chose, chosen

14. spoke, spoken

15. froze, frozen

16. stole, stolen

Review set 52

1. have

2. superlative

3. predicate nominative

4. indirect

5. second

6. plural

7. third, singular

8. adept

9. great

10. protagonist

11. strong

12. loves, transitive

13. sultan, (harem,) palace

14. Aladdin, Mother, I, I

15. of fine jewels, gift

16. three, the, beautiful, the, courageous

17. embarrassed

18. complete sentence

19. phrase

20. (a) turkeys
    (b) charities
    (c) cities

21. know(s), (is) knowing, knew, (has) known

22. tore, torn

23. Dear Majesty,
    You gave me your word that the princess could be my bride. What happened?
    Yours truly,
    Aladdin

24. Princess Badroulboudour, Aladdin's fiancee, accepts his gifts of jewels, servants, and gold.

25. Foreshadowing

26. On January 2, 1992, Mr. and Mrs. Soop welcomed an eight-pound son and named him Brock Lee.

27. him, Aladdin;
    their, people

28. thwarted, magician

29.

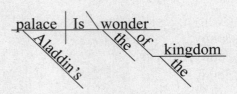

30.

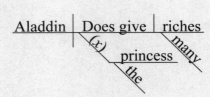

LESSON 53   **Nominative Pronoun Case**

Practice 53

a. S. 1st I
   Sing. 2nd . . you
   S. 3rd (masc.) he
   S. 3rd (fem.) she
   S. 3rd (neuter) it
   Pl. 1st . . . . . we
   Pl. 2nd . . . . you
   Pl. 3rd . . . . they

b. He defeated Nixon in the election.

c. The man at the door was he

d. He and I will run . . . .

e. I, she, they, he, we

f. she

g. they

h. he

i. I

j. Anthropometry

k. anthropo-

l. anthropogenesis

m. anthropomorphous

Review set 53

1. prospective

2. They're

3. perspective

4. before

5. most

6. first

7. second

8. wore

9. stolen

10. (a) lunches
    (b) deer
    (c) lives

11. has been synchronizing, present perfect progressive

12. clause

13. run-on sentence

14. Does sound, linking

15. In, Far East, African

16. sang

17. luckier, luckiest

18. Look under "Pape, Eric" to find other works by this artist

19. Dear Genie,
    I am in treouble. Please help me.
    Gratefully,
    Aladdin

20. of *time;
    on living *organisms

21. disguised

22. exposes, transitive

23. objective case

24. Princess Badroulboudour

25. their, Molly and Kurt;
    them, Molly and Kurt

26. drink, (is) drinking, drank, (has) drunk

27. (a) grew, grown
    (b) bore, borne

28. Having witnessed, perfect tense

29.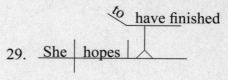

30.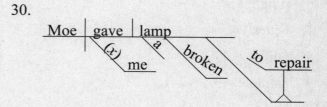

LESSON 54   **Objective Pronoun Case**

Practice 54

a. S. 1st . . . . . me
   S. 2nd . . . . . you
   S. 3rd (masc.) him
   S. 3rd (fem.) her
   S. 3rd (neuter) it
   Pl. 1st . . . . . us
   Pl. 2nd . . . . you
   Pl. 3rd . . . . . them

b. A basket carries her to the moon.

c. A narrator tells us a story

d. Wilda swept cobwebs with him and me

e. . . . to my brother and me.

f. me, him, them, her, us

g. me

h. her

i. them

j. pathos

k. motif

l. narrator

m. figures, speech

Review set 54

1. third

2. case

3. knew

4. grown

5. torn

6. rung

7. better

8. phil-

9. antidote

10. hero

11. angles

12. phrase

13. (a) batteries
    (b) keys
    (c) results

14. has grown, linking

15. has grown, linking

16. Dear Counselor Hegarty,
    Twenty-four years ago today, your son and my son were born at Huntington Memorial Hospital. Are they still friends?
    Warmly,
    Judge Brooke

17. (a) chose, (has) chosen
    (b) took, (has) taken

18. more trustworthy, most trustworthy

19. nominative

20. predicate

21. an accomplished painter

22. Stephanie, my sister-in-law, makes puppets.

23. objective case

24. his, Tiki-Pu;
    his, Tiki-Pu

25. scheming

26. The, bad, Tiki-Pu's, Wio-Wani's

27. hoth, and

28.

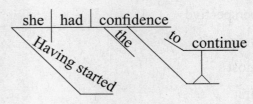

29.

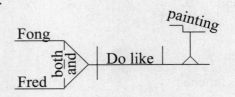

30.

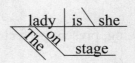

LESSON 55   **Personal Pronoun Case Forms**

Practice 55

a. objective case

b. nominative case

c. possessive case

d. direct objectr

e. possession

f. subject

g. indirect object

h. object of a preposition

i. predicate nominative

j. We

k. me

l. agnostic

m. agnosia

n. diagnosis

o. prognosis

p. gnosis

Review set 55

1. clause

2. angle

3. cliché

4. end

5. humans

6. narrator

7. (a) feet
   (b) inches
   (c) yard

8. might be exploring, transitive

9. At the *age;
   of *eighteen;
   for the *Kansas City Star

10. swear, (is) swearing, swore, (has) sworn

11. less, least

12. Mr. Hemingway died on Sunday, July 2, 1961, a few days before his sixty-second birthday

13. Ernest Hemingway said, "Courage is grace under pressure."

14. and, but, or, nor, for, yet, so

15. were feeling, linking

16. had taught, past perfect

17. Ernest's father

18. his/Dr. Clarence Hemingway

19. phrase

20. S. 1st I
    S. 2nd . . . . . you
    S. 3rd (masc.) he
    S. 3rd (fem.) she
    S. 3rd (neuter) it
    Pl. 1st . . . . . we
    Pl. 2nd . . . you
    Pl. 3rd . . . . . they

21. a, an, the

22. The winner was he.

23. (a) blew, (has) blown
    (b) shrank, (has) shrunk

24. A

25. Having deteriorated

26. hunting, fishing

27.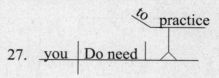

28.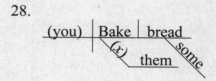

29.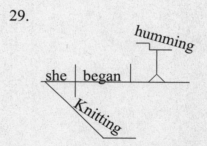

30.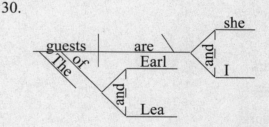

LESSON 56

Possessive Pronouns and Possessive Adjectives • Diagramming Pronouns

Practice 56

a.

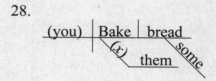

b.

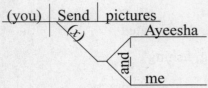

c.

d. its

e. theirs

f. your

g. They're

h. It's

i. paradox

j. dialogue

k. comedy

l. action

More Practice 56

1. their

2. they're

3. its

4. ours

5. hers

6. yours

7. your

8. They're . . . there.

9. its

10. You're

11. they're

12. their

Review set 56

1. run-on sentence

2. worse

3. Does

4. theirs

5. cliché

6. anthropos

7. clever

8. careful

9. No, other, his, the, abundant, the, hidden

10. besides *Ali Baba and his *wife;
about the abundant *treasure;
in the hidden *cave

11. pours, intransitive

12. pours, transitive

13. and, but, or, for, nor, yet, so

14. Neither/nor

15. Long ago, Dr. Habib lived at 1000 East
Oasis Avenue, Cavetown, Persia.

16. Dear Ali Baba Family,
The captain and his forty thieves are
seeking revenge. Please be on your guard
against any strangers.
With concern,
Morgiana

17. Morgiana, a clever and intelligent slave,
saves Ali Baba's life four times.

18. Does seem, linking

19. (a) thieves
(b) alleys
(c) allies

20. *See chart on page 321.*

21. phrase

22. He, nominative case

23. them, objective case

24. (a) froze, (has) frozen
(b) spoke, (has) spoken

25. sing, (is) singing, sang, (has) sung

26. burning, hiding

27. are organizing, present progressive tense

28.

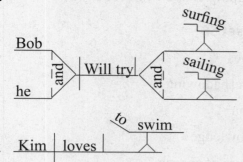

29.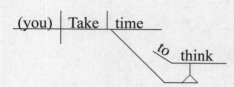

30.

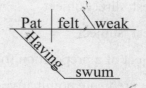

LESSON 57   **Dependent and Independent Clauses • Subordinating Conjunctions**

Practice 57

a. dependent

b. independent

c. independent

d. dependent

e. After

f. even though

g. When

h. poly-

i. polyglot

j. polygraph

k. polytechnic

More Practice 57   *See Master Worksheets*

Review set 57

1. has tired, present perfect

2. *See the chart on page 321.*

3. yours

4. its

5. He

6. Your

7. figure of speech

8. gnosis

9. humans

10. loves

11. faster

12. sung

13. *See the chart on page 321.*

14. promises pages

15. I. Howard Pyle's stories
    A. "How Boots Befooled the King"
    B. "King Stork"
    C. "The Stool of Fortune"

16. clause

17. good; Ex: captivating, enchanting, astonishing, delightful, magnificent, charming, etc.

18. blow, (is) blowing, blew, (has) blown

19. This, the

20. to outsmart, direct object

21. may purchase, transitive

22. objective

23. antecedent

24. nominative

25. Does appear, linking

26. (a) daughters-in-law
    (b) mouthfuls

27. According to my *mother; next to *godliness

28. Ex: The high councilor, the wisest man in the world, is Boots's next victim.

29.

30.

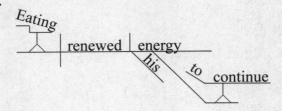

LESSON 58 — Gerunds vs. Participles and Verbs • Gerund Phrases

Practice 58

a. falling action

b. exaggeration

c. autobiography

d. description

e. conflict

f. Hearing the church bells; direct object

g. Collecting unusual stamps; subject

h. Revealing the solution; object of a preposition (before)

i. Biking to the beach; predicate nominative

j. your

k. His

l. my

m. gerund (noun)

n. verb

o. participle (adjective)

More Practice 58

1. painting the eaves of his house; object of a preposition (for)

2. His limping; subject

3. cheating on the test; object of a preposition (of)

4. cheating on the test; direct object

5. cheating on the test; subject

6. living simply; object of a preposition (on)

7. clipping coupons; predicate nominative

8. clipping coupons, direct object

Review set 58

1. loves

2. foreshadowing

3. -gon

4. knowledge

5. figure of speech

6. indirect

7. theirs

8. many

9. stole

10. she

11. sentence fragment

12. phrase

13. Mrs. Sanchez said, "On Saturday, August 3, 2002, I played Chinese checkers, read a French novel, and cleaned my refrigerator.

14. dependent

15. case

16. objective

17. English

18. Has flown, intransitive

19. Has been expecting, present perfect progressive tense

20. and, but, or, for, nor, yet, so

21. Does smell, linking

22. (a) women
    (b) babies
    (c) days

23. throw, (is) throwing, three, (has) thrown

24. so that I can play tomorrow

25. B

26. Examples: Can Daisy and I help him? Can I help Daisy and him (him and Daisy)?

27. Having failed, perfect tense

28. to study

29.

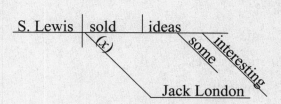

30.

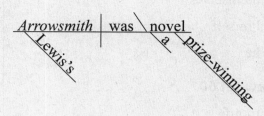

LESSON 59   **Participial Phrases • Diagramming Participial and Gerund Phrases**

Practice 59

a. borne

b. born

c. born

d. borne

e. hiding under the rock, modifies "snake"

f. Exiting the theater, modifies "crowd."

g. painted by her favorite artist, modifies "lighthouse"

h. drawn in pencil, modifies "one"

i.

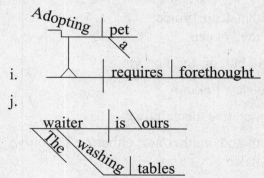

j.

More Practice 59   *See Master Worksheets*

Review set 59

1. anecdote

2. worn

3. religion

4. epic

5. yours

6. cliché

7. gerund

8. him

9. purer

10.   (a) Freddys
    (b) daddies
    (c) sons-in-law

11. stubborn, greedy, rude

12. has been trying, present perfect progressive tense

13. have broken

14. has been spinning

15. Correlative

16. nominative case

17. phrase

18. line transitive

19. Can remain, linking verb

20. break, (is) breaking, broke, (has) broken

21. Dear Dr. Paine,
On MOnday, October 8, 2001, you filled a cavity in my tooth. It still hurts.
Regretfully,
Miss Sniffle

22. Howard Pyle, an American illustrator and writer, wrote a story called "The Stool of Fortune."

23. them

24. her/princess

25. her

26. false

27. After he found the princess

28.

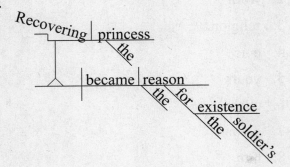

29.

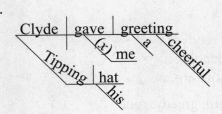

30.

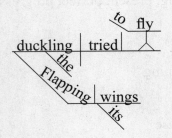

LESSON 60   Reflexive and Intensive Pronouns

Practice 60

a. I

b. himself

c. You

d. themselves

e. We (ourselves) | rocked | babies
                           the

f. pseudoinvalid

g. pseudo

h. pseudonym

i. pseudoclassic

More Practice 60

1. himself

2. themselves

3. themselves

4. I

5. me

6. themselves

7. himself

8. themselves

9. himself

10. he

Review set 60

1. motif

2. autobiography

3. paradox

4. poly-

5. many

6. first

7. second

8. he

9. hers

10. (a) lice
   (b) Amys
   (c) coaches

11. Your uncle and I attended a lecture about Mars at the observatory in Griffith Park last Tuesday, the eleventh of June

12. with a deep *voice;
to the *queen

13. and, but, or, for, nor, yet, so

14. Do stay, linking

15. imperative, declarative

16. both/and; neither/nor; either/or; not only/but also

17. she, nominative case

18. Does cloud, transitive

19. clause

20. even though it was raining

21. B

22. sentence fragment

23. your, his, its, their

24. our

26. brightest

27. Sylvester, a guitarist, played for our music festival last Sunday

28.

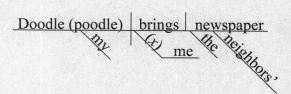

29.

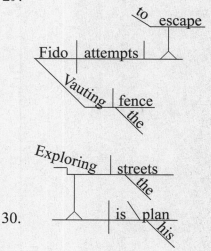

30.

LESSON 61   **The Comma, Part 4: Descriptive Adjectives, Dependent Clauses**

Practice 61

a. The brilliant, ingenious Sir Isaac Newton was an English mathematician and scientist.

b. The young, motivated scientist conceived the idea of universal gravitation at the age of twenty-five.

c. Common white light is really a mixture of all other colors. (*no comma to separate color adjective "white"*)

d. Because he formulated our theories of physics, Sir Isaac Newton is recognized as one fo the greatest geniuses of all time.

e. Even though Newton explained rainbows, they remain a mystery to me.

f. While he is most famous for the law of universal gravitation, he also built the first reflecting telescope.

g. didactic

h. connotations

i. denotation

j. allusion

More Practice 61   *See Master Worksheets*

Review set 61

1. loves

2. paradox

3. many

4. borne

5. me

6. himself

7. third

8. him

9. theirs, ours

10. (a) batteries
    (b) attorneys-at-law
    (c) dishes

11. Mr. Cod's seafood recipe, I believe, calls for one pound of shrimp, three pounds of halibut, and three ounces of Wisconsin cheese.

12. On September 21, 1902, Mrs. Shade planted a peach tree at 2091 Spruce Street, Oak City, West Virginia.

13. According to the *newspaper; throughout the *week

14. herself

15. imperative

16. Old Pipes was the kind of person whom everyone respected

17. me, objective case

18. Is walking, intransitive

19. and, but, or, for, nor, yet, so

20. (Although) David is wearing a raincoat, he is still getting quite wet.

21. Are living, present progressive tense

22. run-on sentence

23. recapturing the beautiful Dryad

24. Sal's

25. happier

26. blow, (is) blowing, blew, (has) blown

27. Stephen, an avid philatelist, collects Scandinavian postage stamps.

28.

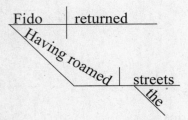

29.

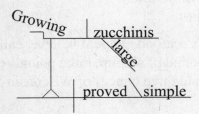

30.

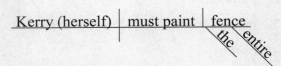

LESSON 62   Compound Sentences • Coordinating Conjunctions

Practice 62

a. simple

b. compound; and

c. compound; so

d. compound; but

e. simple

f.

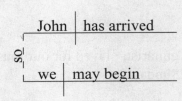

g. pathos

h. apathy

i. sympathy

j. empathy

k. antipathy

Review set 62

1. conflict

2. pseudo

3. Connotation

4. Didactic

5. I

6. themselves

7. him, me

8. he

9. yours

10. sung

11. (a) trenches
    (b) territories
    (c) properties

12. The green, shaggy, merry followers of Robin Hood enjoyed life to the fullest. They sang songs, ate venison, and played games in the forests of England.

13. from between the *trees; in the *grove

14. (a) could smell, action
    (b) may have smelled, linking

15. phrase

16. That type of collie likes to herd.

17. they, nominative case: Little John, Robin Hood

18. Did defeat, transitve

19. both/and; neither/nor; either/or, not only/but also

20. (unless) he knocked Little John off the bridge

21. (when) he met Little John

22. B

23. hiding in the surrounding trees

24. his

25. most delightful

26. drink, (is) drinking, drank, (has) drunk

27. us

28.

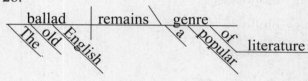

29.

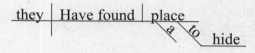

30.

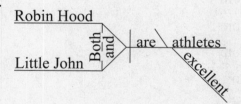

LESSON 63   The Comma, Part 5: Compound Sentences, Direct Quotations

Practice 63

a. and, but, or, for, nor, yet, so

b. for

c. yet

d. and

e. The Hebrew word *shalom* means "peace," but it is also used as a greeting or farewell.

f. Father took Mother on a vacation to Holland, for he knew it was her fondest dream.

g. The music teacher asked, "Does anyone know the name of John Philip Sousa's first band?"

h. "At the age of thirteen," the teacher continued, "John Philip Sousa played in the Marine Band, the official band of the President of the United States."

i. archaic

j. slang

k. diction

l. colloquial

m. profane

n. trite

o. vulgar

More Practice 63   *See Master Worksheets*

Review set 63

1. false

2. born

3. denotation

4. Dialogue

5. philanthropist

6. themselves

7. me

8. she

9. false

10. stole

11. glasses

12. Uncle Nigel and Aunt Catherine are proud of their Scottish ancestry. They play bagpipes, eat mutton, and roam the highlands every summer.

13. clause

14. Does sound, linking

15. On behalf of *Robin Hood;
    along the *way

16. complete sentence

17. demands, transitive

18. he, nominative case: man (antecedent)

19. and, but, or, for, nor, yet, so

20. (whenever) he hears a siren

21. Last summer, Jenny read *Beowulf*, and epic
    poem.

22. Having discovered the reason for Allen a
    Dale's unhappiness, perfect tense

23. taking pictures of the sunset

24. theif

25. more helpful

26. choose, (is) choosing, chose, (has) chosen

27. compound sentence, but

28. simple sentence

29.

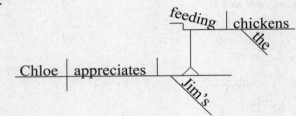

30.

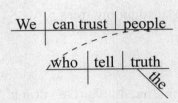

Practice 64

a. who

b. whom

c. whomever

d. that

e. whom

f.

We | can trust | people
who | tell | truth
          the

g. bibliophile

h. biblioclast

i. biblio

j. bibliography

More Practice 64

1. who

2. who

3. whom

4. whom

5. whom

6. who

7. who

8. who

Review set 64

1. custom

2. caricature

3. many

4. moral

5. pathos

6. himself

7. were

8. he

9. yours

10. grown

11. begun

12. my

13. coordinating

14. Nettie said, "If you help me, we can capture all these Jerusalem crickets before Colonel Kleen arrives on Friday."

15. Dear Robin Hood,
    Although you are an excellent archer, the friar is even better. You can visit him, for he lives nearby.
    Sincerely,
    Will Scadlock

16. phrase

17. your or yours

18. Have emerged, intransitive

19. them, yeoman

20. (a) antennae or antennas
    (b) knives
    (c) theories

21. As soon as the white flag waves

22. Hester often uses clichés, overused phrases, in her writing.

23. Having invented a new type of camera, father

24. himself

25. smoothest

26. tear, (is) tearing, tore, (has) torn

27. compound sentences, for

28. simple sentence

29.

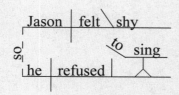

30.

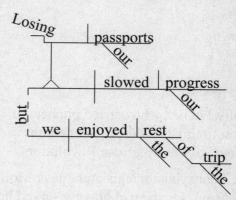

LESSON 65   **The Comma, Part 6: Nonessential Parts • *That* or *Which***

Practice 65

a. bonanza

b. bene, bonus

c. bonus

d. benefactor

e. benevolent

f. nonessential

g. essential

h. nonessential

i. that

j. that

k. which

l. which

Review set 65

1. allusions

2. feelings

3. Antipathy

4. words

5. Colloquial

6. themselves

7. I

8. they

9. who

10. known

11. his

12. dependent

13. Molly Pitcher, who carried pitchers of water to thirsty soldiers, is a famous heroine of the American Revolution.

14. The Pennsylvania legislature gave Molly a pension, for she had bravely served her country.

15. sentence fragment

16. we

17. (a) felt, linking
    (b) felt, action

18. they, nominative case

19. (a) Jameses
    (b) Ortizes
    (c) Jerrys

20. Since it had rained

21. has thrown

22. The expression "busy as a beaver" is a cliché, a trite form of diction.

23. challenging each other, present tense

24. "carrying pitchers of water" modifies lady

25. more unusual

26. freeze, (is) freezing, froze, (has) frozen

27. compound sentence, but

28. simple sentence

29.

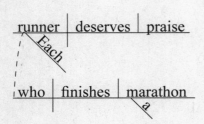

30.

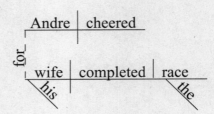

LESSON 66

Pronound Usage: Appositions and Comparisons

Practice 66

a. We

b. us

c. us

d. I

e. we

f. empathy

g. farce

h. analogy

i. context

j. irony

More Practice 66

1. she

2. We

3. us

4. she

5. him

6. she

7. he

8. they

9. We

10. us

Review set 66

1. Empathy

2. antipathy

3. Slang

4. book

5. allusion

6. nonessential

7. he

8. whom

9. he

10. We

11. who

12. Whom

13. my

14. nominative

15. Father Serra, a Franciscan priest, actively assisted the indigenous population in the Southwest.

16. On Monday, August fifth, Col. Brett Jones will meet Davy Crockett at the United States Army base in Saint Louis, Missouri

17. their

18. galloped, intransitive

19. Because of his *fame,
    after his *death,
    about *Davy

20. (a) leaves
    (b) branches
    (c) berries

21. Although he sometimes rides wild horses

22. had spoken

23. Does Davy tame a buffalo?

24. "catching trout" modifies bear

25. best

26. drop, (is) dropping, dropped, (has) dropped

27. essential

28.

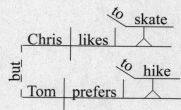

29.

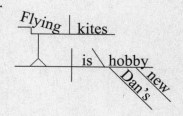

30.

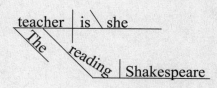

LESSON 67   **Interrogative Pronouns**

Practice 67

a. what

b. Which

c. Whose

d. whom

e. Whose

f. Who

g. interrogative pronoun

h. adjective

i. centimeters

j. metron

k. thermometer

l. altimeter

m. barometer

More Practice 67

1. Who's

2. Whose

3. Who

4. whom

5. Whom

6. Who's

7. Whose

8. whom

9. Who

10. Whom

Review set 67

1. Born

2. Apathy

3. Profane

4. books

5. good

6. I

7. me

8. whom

9. We

10. Whose

11. she

12. which

13. his

14. objetive

15. Dear Mr. Crockett,
Unfortunately, your bear growled Tuesday morning, so my hen refused to lay eggs. If this continues, I will take you to court.
Your neighbor,
Mr. Grump

16. Death Hug, Davy Crockett's pet bear, weighs four hundred fifty pounds and stands six feet tall.

17. me

18. nonessential

19. Does sound, linking

20. (a) Davys
    (b) Commanders in Chief

21. ⟨since⟩ he was a congressman

22. was blowing

23. clause

24. hunting buffalo, deer, and elk

25. worse

26. shrink, (is) shrinking, shrank, (has) shrunk

27. "Bragging about the hurricane" modifies Ben Hardin

28.
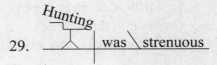

29. Hunting was strenuous

30. The teacher has retired who taught (x) me to read

LESSON 68

Quotation Marks, Part 1

Practice 68

a. none

b. none

c. "Yes," the docent replied, "and Daniel Webster defended the Federalists' principles eloquently."

d. "In addition," said the guid, "Daniel Webster delivered the famous Plymouth and Bunker Hill speeches."

e. software

f. database

g. network

h. hardware

More Practice 68   *See Master Worksheets*

Review set 68

1. connotation

2. empathy

3. generous

4. good

5. irony

6. they

7. me

8. who

9. We

10. theirs

11. that

12. whom

13. my

14. which

15. Dear Mr. Grump,
Bears growl, and roosters crow.
If you will silence your rooster, I will
silence my bear.
Your neighbor,
Davy Crockett

16. I. Davy Crockett's pets
A. The bear
B. The alligator
C. The cougar

17. you

18. either/or, neither/nor, not only/but also,
both/and

19. might prove, action

20. essential

21. (Although) most of Davy Crockett's
legends are wild exaggerations

22. had shrunk

23. phrase

24. "You can lead a horse to water," said
Grandma, "but you can't make it drink."

25. more euphonic

26. wear, (is) wearing, wore, (has) worn

27. "Using his creativity" modifies Davy

28.

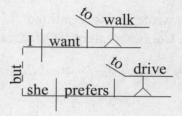

29.

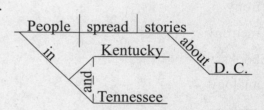

30.

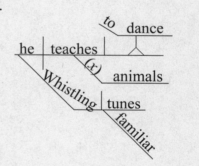

LESSON
69

Quotation Marks, Part 2

Practice 69

a. chroma

b. monochrome

c. polychrome

d. chromosome

e. "Well," said the father bullfrog, as he sucked in as much air as he could, "he couldn't have been much bigger than this."
"But he really was much bigger than that," replied the young bullfrog.
"Okay son, watch me now. He couldn't possibly have been bigger than this."

f. In "The Bull and the Bullfrog," the old bullfrog puffed himself up so big that he burst into tiny pieces!

g. Have you heard the song "Climb Every Mountain"?

h. Mark Twain wrote an essay entitled "Fennimore Cooper's Literary Offenses."

More Practice 69   *See Master Worksheets*

Review set 69

1. irony
2. metron
3. books
4. analogy
5. analogy
6. I
7. I
8. fastest
9. us
10. yours
11. that
12. which
13. my
14. which
15. who
16. Dear Mr. Crockett,
On Friday, September 24, 1834, Judge Snikity will be in town, so we can setle our dispute.
Meet me at the courthouse at ten a.m. sharp, or risk a jail sentence.

Your neighbor,
Mr. Grump

17. I
18. Don, a United States citizen, served twelve years as a consul in Panama.
19. Had frozen, intransitive
20. As cold temperatures ravaged the earth
21. (a) stitches
    (b) cherries
22. nonessential
23. phrase
24. Davy Crockett sang a song called "Fire in the Mountain."
25. worst
26. grin, (is) grinning, grinned, (has) grinned
27. "roping steer" modifies frontiersmen
28.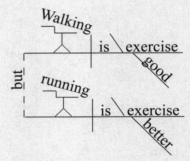
29.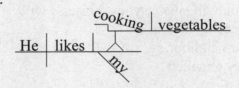
30.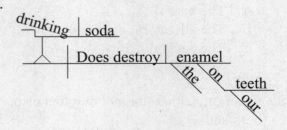

Practice 70

a. genres

b. gothic novel

c. epithet

d. flashback

e. drama

f. This

g. Those

h. This

i. These

j. This

k. pointing

Review set 70

1. measure

2. measures

3. Hardware

4. benevolent

5. database

6. I

7. I

8. ours

9. braver

10. us

11. who

12. which

13. that

14. has begun, present perfect tense

15. B

16. Dear Mr. Grump,
    By Friday, September 24, 1834, I will no longer reside in this territory.
    I am headed for the wild West, and I will take my pets with me.

Sincerely,
Crockett

17. they

18. "Daniel Boone's Rifle," a short story by Stewart Edward, tells about two young men who learn to appreciate what they have.

19. Does seem, linking

20. even though she had lived a long time

21. (a) mothers-in-law
    (b) stepfathers

22. are worrying

23. clause

24. "I think," said Russell, "that Daniel Boone gave his rifle to Mr. Burnett."

25. most hilarious

26. empty, (is) emptying, emptied, (has) emptied

27. "Having read the story about Daniel Boone" modifies Grandma

28.

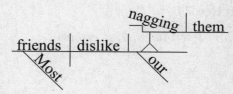

29.

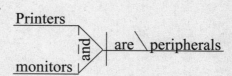

30.

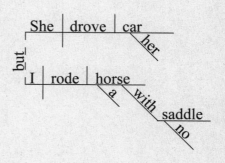

Practice 71

a. all, plural

b. Nothing, singular

c. want

d. are

e. has

f. follow, their

g. deserves, its

h. tries, his/her

i. pachyderm

j. derma

k. melanoderm

l. taxidermy

m. dermatology

n. epidermis

More Practice 71

S = singular; P = plural; E = either

1. E

2. P

3. S

4. S

5. S

6. E

7. S

8. P

9. S

10. P

11. S

12. P

13. S

14. S

15. P

16. E

17. S

18. P

19. E

20. E

Review set 71

1. hardware

2. chroma

3. color

4. measures

5. interconnected

6. me

7. he

8. Whose

9. that

10. we

11. my

12. himself

13. Those

14. wants

15. In a short story called "The Round Table," Arthur requires his knights to be present at five p.m. for an early supper.

16. Had succeeded, past perfect tense

17. them

18. The author, Beatrice Clay, tells about Arthur's birth and his rise to kingship.

19. essential

20. (Since) Sir Kay had no sword

21. looked, linking

22. looked, action

23. had misplaced

24. phrase

25. quieter

26. steal, (is) stealing, stole, (has) stolen

27. "Looking for his sword" modifies Sir Kay

28.
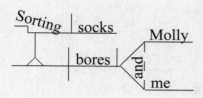

29.
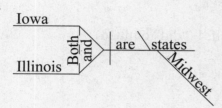

30.
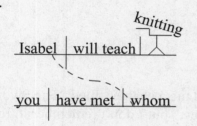

LESSON 72   Italics or Underline

Practice 72

a. stereotype

b. pun

c. stream of consciousness

d. soliloquy

e. satire

f. Traditional Homes

g. you know

h. gastrocnemius

i. Feliz Navidad

j. Titanic

More Practice 72   *See Master Worksheets*

Review set 72

1. pseudoinvalid

2. place

3. Software

4. color

5. epithet

6. he, themselves

7. I

8. brushes, his/her

9. which

10. us

11. his

12. those

13. likes

14. Each day before class begins, the seventh graders at Cleminson School sing a song called "America the Beautiful."

15. "Unfortunately," said James, "I missed my flight from Chicago to New York City, so I took the train instead."

16. had injured, past perfect

17. we

18. Jumbo the elephant is a pachyderm, an animal with thick skin.

19. nonessential

20. when he resisted Lady Annoure's offers of power and wealth

21. were jousting, intransitive

22. either, singular

23. himself

24. sentence fragment

25. better

26. slip, (is) slipping, slipped, (has) slipped

27. Using soliloquies modifies "Beatrice Clay"

28. <u>Bonjour</u>

29.

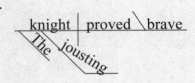

30.

knight | proved \brave
The / jousting

LESSON 73   Irregular Verbs, Part 3

Practice 73

a. bit, (has) bitten

b. dragged, (has) dragged

c. fought, (has) fought

d. flew; (has) flown

e. fled; (has) fled

f. drove, (has) driven

g. dove, (has) dived

h. built, (has) built

i. beat

j. brought

k. driven

l. cost

m. fell

n. built

o. autograph

p. automobile

q. autobiography

r. auto-

s. automatic

More Practice 73   *See Master Worksheets*

Review set 73

1. color

2. database

3. genres

4. derma

5. denotation

6. him

7. himself, I ("did" omitted)

8. plural

9. that

10. us

11. his

12. theirs

13. is

14. Mom read me a chapter titled "The Sword in the Stone," but I don't remember it, for I was sleeping.

15. "Yes," said Andy, "Ms. Williams read that chapter to me last Saturday."

16. relies

17. us

18. were fighting, past progressive tense

19. nonessential

20. even though the Archbishop of Canterbury has declared Arthur king

21. King Arthur, concrete; towns, concrete; order, abstract

22. several, plural

23. Because of King Arthur's *proposal; to the *marriage; of *Arthur and *Guinevere

24. phrase

25. most studious

26. bring, (is) bringing, brought, (has) brought

27. to stay

28. <u>The Thinker</u>

29.

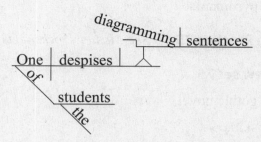

30.

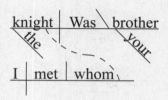

LESSON 74   **Irregular Verbs, Part 4**

Practice 74

a. went, (has) gone

b. hid, (has) hidden

c. lost, (has) lost

d. made, (has) made

e. ran, (has) run

f. rode, (has) ridden

g. raised, (has) raised

h. mistook, (has) mistaken

i. led

j. went

k. made

l. put

m. understatement

n. plagiarism

o. resolution

p. slapstick

q. slice of life

More Practice 74   *See Master Worksheets*

Review set 74

1. books

2. analogy

3. context

4. colors

5. flashback

6. who

7. whom

8. wants, his/her

9. which

10. We

11. our

12. This

13. whom

14. brought

15. When Mom read me the chapter called "The Candle in the Wind," I was wide awake.

16. "As a matter of fact," said Andy, "I have never heard that part of King Arthur's story."

17. our

18. everybody, singular

19. nonessential

20. (that) most of the stories surrounding . . . are fabrications

21. must have been gleaming, intransitive

22. all, none, any, some, most

23. Having received pardon from King Arthur, perfect tense

24. sentence fragment

25. (a) tankfuls
     (b) Justices of the Peace
     (c) entities

26. build, (is) building, built, (has) built

27. *The Starry Night*, one of Van Gogh's paintings, shows a village under the night sky in southern France.

28. <u>Bridge Over a Pool of Water Lilies</u>

29.

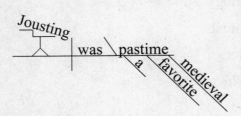

30.

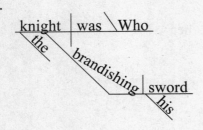

LESSON 75   **Irregular Verbs, Part 5**

Practice 75

a. set, (has) set

b. shone, (has) shined

c. shined, (has) shined

d. shut, (has) shut

e. slept, (has) slept

f. sprang, (has) sprung

g. sat

h. took

i. taught

j. told

k. written

l. woken

m. striven

n. swum

o. pyrotechnics

p. pyrography

q. pyrogen

r. pyro-

s. pyromaniac

More Practice 75   *See Master Worksheets*

Review set 75

1. gothic novel

2. skins

3. skin

4. pun

5. Satire

6. whom

7. whom

8. needs, his/her

9. that

10. We

11. Jenny's

12. Those

13. hers

14. dove

15. Collecting his horse, his armor, and his sword, Arthur prepares for battle.

16. "Last Monday," said James, "I flew from Chicago, Illinois, to Sacramento, California."

17. his

18. Much, singular

19. nonessential clause

20. himself

21. to emulate, adjective (modifies "knight")

22. faithful, trustworthy

23. Playing softly in the background modifies "mandolinists"

24. he, Sir Lancelot

25. less

26. eat, 9is) eating, ate, (has) eaten

27. Queen Victoria, a great monarch of Great Britain, reigned from 1837 until her death in 1901.

28. <u>Taraxacum officinale</u>

29.

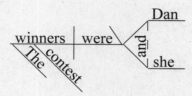

30.

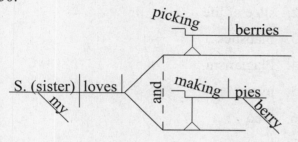

LESSON 76 **The Exclamation Mark • The Question Mark • The Dash**

Practice 76

a. Wow! Look at the "Big Dipper"!

b. Do you know another name for Ursa Minor?

c. Is it "Little Dipper"?

d. Brilliant! You know your constellations!

e. At one time, Rudolph Valentino was a famous actor—the heartthrob of millions . . . .

f. . . . roles in the two motion pictures—let me think—*The Four Horsemen* . . . .

g. "Hold on to your—" said Gary as the wind swept Mary's hat from her head.

h. point

i. first

j. third

k. person

l. limited

m. unlimited

n. camera

More Practice 76   *See "Slapstick Story #4 in Master Worksheets.*

Review set 76

1. puns

2. skin

3. pun

4. auto-

5. understatement

6. Whoever

7. whomever

8. wants, her

9. which

10. us

11. Petey's

12. Those

13. yours

14. bitten

15. If we have time, we shall read the chapter entitled "The Adventure of the Chapel Perilous."

16. "No," said Ms. Sweet, "I did not leave my gundrops in the tent."

17. her, hers

18. (a) Has proved, action
    (b) Did prove, linking

19. essential

20. phrase

21. mending the tent

22. complete sentence

23. had come

24. (If)Sir Lancelot du Lac had kissed the Lady of the Chapel Perilous

25. evil

26. fall, (is) falling, fell, (has) fallen

27. According to the *Lady;
    of the *Chapel Perilous

28. <u>Queen Mary</u>

29.

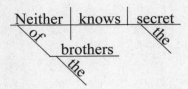

30.

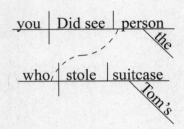

LESSON 77

Subject-Verb Agreement, Part 1

Practice 77

a. derives

b. exceed

c. differ

d. are

e. exists

f. make

g. cosmopolis

h. microcosm

i. macrocosm

j. Cosmos

k. cosmonaut

l. cosmopolitan

More Practice 77

1. sound

2. are

3. live

4. grow

5. are

6. love

7. was

8. were

9. were

10. have

Review set 77

1. self

2. slice of life

3. Slapstick

4. Plagiarism

5. pyro-

6. who

7. her

8. has, its

9. that

10. We

11. Kerry's

12. Those

13. their

14. taken

15. "Help!" yelled Tom. "Did you see who stole my suitcase?"

16. "Did the Portuguese lady with whom you spoke see the thief?" asked Tom

17. your, yours

18. Has unhorsed, transitive

19. nonessential clause

20. his, Sir Gareth

21. to read, adjective

22. most pleasant

23. Some, singular

24. (when) he wins the heart of Lady Liones

25. tell, (is) telling, told, (has) told

26. Lady Linit, Lady Liones's sister, marries Sir Gaheris.

27. (a) shelves
(b) matches
(c) ladies

28. The Last Battle

29.

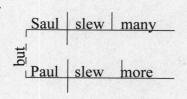

30.

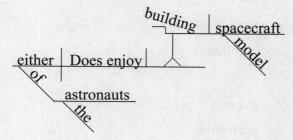

LESSON 78   **Subject-Verb Agreement, Part 2**

Practice 78

a. descriptions | were

b. Cornelius V. | was

c. list | is

d.
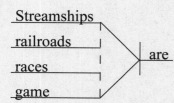

e. epigram

f. dramatic monologue

g. antithesis

h. action

i. essay

More Practice 78

1. sits
2. smells
3. is
4. go
5. are
6. drives
7. makes
8. was
9. live
10. flies

Review set 78

1. fire
2. self
3. army on horseback
4. resolution
5. third
6. whomever
7. she
8. trusts, his/her
9. which
10. us
11. my
12. eats
13. hers
14. mistaken
15. Sir Lancelot, one of King Arthur's knights, admits to Sir Gareth, "You are a stout knight."

16. Dear King Arthur,
    Thank you for granting me my three
    requests. How excited I am to be a knight!
    Sir Lancelot knighted me.
    Gratefully,
    Sir Gareth

17. and, but, or, for, nor, yet, so

18. Does appear, linking

19. essential clause

20. phrase

21. to prepare, noun

22. nominative, objective, and possessive cases

23. Each, singular

24. (that) represented Christian purity
    during medieval times

25. go, (is) going, went, (has) gone

26. Grieving the lost and wounded modifies
    "King Arthur"

27. of *warriors,
    alongside of the *Red Knight

28. <u>Los Angeles Times</u>

29.
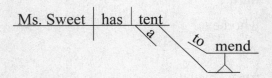

30.
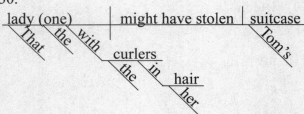

LESSON   Subject-Verb Agreement,
79   Part 3

Practice 79

a. isn't

b. allow

c. aren't

d. There are

e. differs

f. therapy

g. therapeutic index

h. therap

i. therapeutic

j. therapist

More Practice 79

1. help

2. have

3. isn't

4. complains

5. pays

6. expects

7. performs

8. hopes

9. obeys

10. prefers

11. wraps

12. doesn't

13. doesn't

14. aren't

15. isn't

Review Set 79

1. first-person

2. fires

3. plagiarism

4. pun

5. cosmos

6. Who

7. me

8. knows, her

9. who

10. we

11. his

12. sit

13. their

14. ridden

15. During the 1930s, millions of Americans lost their jobs, their homes, and their financial security.

16. "Unfortunately," said Grandfather Lucius, "The stock market crashed, so my investments became worthless."

17. Playing the stock moarket

18. had been appearing, past perfect progressive tense

19. nonessential clause

20. run-on sentence

21. worse

22. us

23. some, plural

24. he, Monty

25. give, (is) giving, gave, (has) given

26. Sir Galahad, king of Sarras, rules in faraway Babylon.

27. (a) archetypes
    (b) waxes
    (c) elves

28. Ivanhoe

29.

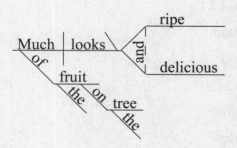

30.

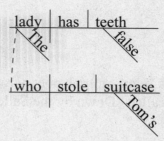

LESSON 80   Subject-Verb Agreement, Part 4

Practice 80

a. remains

b. causes

c. is

d. captures

e. dress

f. has

g. holds

h. figurative language

i. local color

j. exposition

k. impressionism

Review Set 80

1. understatement

2. self

3. burning

4. unlimited

5. world

6. Whom

7. him and me

8. Was, his/her

9. that

10. us

11. his

12. sees

13. hers

14. lain

15. There are

16. William Butler Yeats, an Irish poet, wrote a short ballad called "Down by the Salley Gardens."

17. Entering the spacecraft, modifies "cosmonaut"

18. Does grant, transitive

19. essential

20. (after) Estorause died

21. worst

22. them

23. one, singular

24. to sing, noun

25. shake, (is) shanking, shook, (has) shaken

26. According to *rumors,
    of the *city,
    of *Sarras,
    into the *dungeon

27. phrase

28. <u>National Geographic</u>

29.
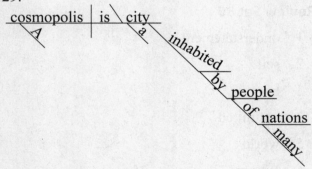

30.
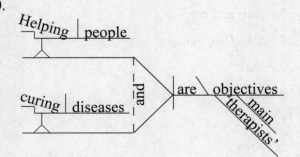

Practice 81

a. ever

b. could

c. anything

d. ever

e. any

f. hydrogen

g. hydrophobia

h. Hydraulic

i. hydrants

j. hydra

k. dehydrate

More Practice 81

1. a

2. anything

3. anywhere

4. anything

5. any

6. any

7. ever

8. any

9. anyone

10. either

Review set 81

1. limited

2. world

3. opposite

4. epigram

5. therap-

6. whom

7. He and I, you and him

8. is, his/her
9. which
10. We
11. our
12. wants
13. doesn't, yours
14. swum
15. are
16. "All right," replied Jim, "I will practice the cello, feed the fish, and wash the dishes while you, Mom, are vacationing in Wisconsin."
17. fighting with people
18. had been searching, past perfect progressive
19. essential clause
20. (after) it has gone to sleep
21. more generous
22. they
23. much, singular
24. he, Mr. Hake
25. sleep, (is) sleeping, slept, (has) slept
26. Piet Mondrian, a Dutch artist known for his nonrepresentational art, painted *Broadway Boogie-Woogie* to express his reactions to the world around him
27. (a) Harrys
    (b) babies
    (c) sons-in-law
28. <u>S</u>, Sirs
29.
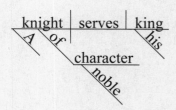

30.
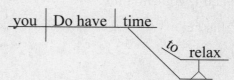

LESSON 82   The Hyphen: Compund Nouns, Numbers

Practice 82

a. narrator
b. moral
c. myth
d. narration
e. malapropism
f. Twenty-one, thirty-one, fifty-two
g. check-in
h. twenty-four, thirty-two
i. thirteen-year-old
j. ninety-eight

More Practice 82

1. twenty-six
2. forty-four
3. eighty-one
4. thirty-nine
5. 97-94
6. follow-up
7. carry-on
8. up-and-down

Review set 82

1. cure
2. metaphor
3. figurative language
4. feelings
5. hydra-
6. participle

7. She and I, you and him

8. has, his/her

9. any

10. I

11. my

12. cheers

13. Weren't

14. woven

15. himself

16. In Westminster, England, King Arthur and Queen Guinevere discover a letter dated Wednesday, September 3, 1250.

17. to dream, noun

18. had been mistaken, past perfect tense

19. nonessential clause

20. (even though) I had drunk plenty of water

21. both/and, either/or, neither/nor, not only/ but also

22. it

23. most, singular

24. of *King Arthur,
    onto his *jealousy and *rage,
    towards *Lancelot

25. run, (is) running, ran, (has) run

26. Does look, linking

27. sentence fragment

28. Broadway Boogie-Woogie

29.

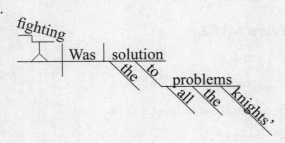

30.

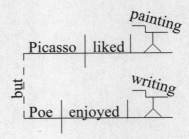

LESSON 83   **Adverbs that Tell "How"**

Practice 83

a. "Violently" and "frequently" modify "erupts."

b. "Explosively" and "forcefully" modify "spew."

c. "Quietly" and "continually" modify "erupt

d. adjective, modifies "Jen"

e. adverbs, modify "wrote"

f. adjective, modifies "bust"

g. adverb, modifies "revealed"

h. psychosis

i. psychic

j. psychotherapy

k. psychology

l. psyche

Review set 83

1. water

2. first-

3. world

4. bravery

5. malapropism

6. negatives

7. they

8. has, its

9. ever

10. He and I, she

11. us

12. is

13. was

14. saw

15. I

16. "Half of my class has already completed the first twenty-five lessons of the English grammar book," said Mrs. Smith.

17. Sleeping peacefully modifies "maiden"

18. were riding, past progressive tense

19. essential

20. (when) Sir Lancelot refused to fight back

21. (a) shovelfuls
    (b) staffs
    (c) axes

22. him

23. some, singular

24. tastiest

25. lose, (is) losing, lost, (has) lost

26. Is crying, intransitive

27. run-on sentence

28. <u>Camelot</u>

29.

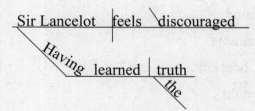

30.

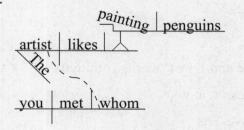

Practice 84

a. well

b. good

c. well

d. good

e. well

f. plot line

g. realism

h. parable

i. poetry

j. parallelism

More Practice 84

1. good

2. well

3. well

4. good

5. good

6. well

7. well

8. good

9. well

10. good

Review set 84

1. malapropism

2. water

3. psyche

4. Exposition

5. Point of view

6. adverbs

7. She and I, he

8. our

9. themselves

10. Aren't

11. hers, doesn't, theirs

12. whom

13. that

14. eaten

15. taller

16. Last Tuesday, Dr. Getz spent forty-five minutes reading us his favorite short story about King Arthur. Its title was "How King Arthur and Sir Gawain Went to France".

17. (a) gerund
    (b) participle
    (c) verb

18. Has ridden, present perfect tense

19. nonessential

20. (Before) Sir Gawain dies

21. and, but, or, for, nor, yet, so

22. he

23. (a) adverb
    (b) adjective

24. she, Debby

25. catch, (is) catching, caught, (has) caught

26. phrase

27. In spite of the *thunderstorm,
    throughout the *night,
    across the *desert,
    to Mom's *hometown

28. Beowulf

29.

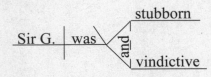

30.

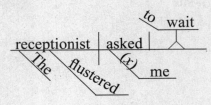

LESSON 85   **The Hyphen: Compound Adjectives**

Practice 85

a. PG 13-rated

b. pro-American, American-made

c. self-appointed, re-signed

d. none

e. six-yard

f. thermometer

g. thermos

h. hypothermia

i. hyperthermia

j. thermostat

k. thermos

Review set 85

1. water

2. malapropism

3. mind

4. parable

5. Local color

6. could

7. is

8. has

9. We

10. She and I, he ("works" omitted)

11. doesn't, any

12. leaves, its

13. them

14. driven

15. me

16. "This recipe," said Aunt Bea, "calls for three and three-fourths cups of well-sifted flour. It makes twenty-four pancakes."

17. (a) gerund
    (b) participle
    (c) verb

18. was attacking, past progressive tense

19. nonessential clause

20. (as soon as) I find Tom's suitcase

21. (a) Curtises
    (b) sheaves
    (c) fathers-in-law

22. she

23. (a) adverb
    (b) adjective

24. Grandpa frequently tells me his favorite old saying, "A rolling stone gathers no moss."

25. cost, (is) costing, cost, (has) cost

26. tastier

27. to forgive, adjective; to forget, adjective

28. <u>New York Times</u>

29.

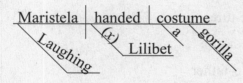

30.

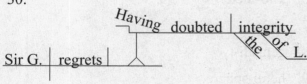

LESSON 86   **Adverbs that Tell "Where"**

Practice 86

a. "inside" modifies <u>lumbered</u>

b. "nowhere" modifies <u>has gone</u>

c. "there" modifies <u>might have been working</u>

d. "around" modifies <u>scampered</u>

e.

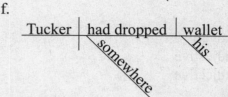

f.

Tucker | had dropped | wallet — his, somewhere

g. rising action

h. sarcasm

i. romance

j. symbol

k. structure

Review set 86

1. malapropism

2. water

3. pun

4. lazy

5. mind

6. good

7. he and I, her

8. my

9. I

10. isn't

11. yours, doesn't, hers

12. who

13. which

14. ridden

15. most

16. "Excuse me, Dad, but isn't this a self-cleaning oven?" asked Tom.

17. (a) participle
    (b) verb
    (c) gerund

18. had desired, past perfect tense

19. essential

20. (while) Tom was not looking

21. Most, plural

22. you

23. (a) adverb
    (b) adjective
    (c) adjective

24. phrase

25. feel, (is) feeling, felt, (has) felt

26. In addition to *Sir Bedivere,
    around *King Arthur,
    during his *time,
    of *need

27. to explore, adjective

28. <u>déjà vu</u>

29.

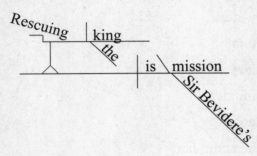

30.

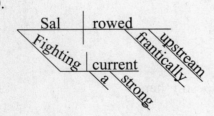

LESSON 87 Word Division

Practice 87

a. in-ept

b. ori-gin

c. coa-li-tion

d. none

e. none

f. forty-nine

g. Physiology

h. Physiometry

i. physiognomy

k. physiocrat

More Practice 87

1. none

2. none

3. sub-stance

4. none

5. hemo-glo-bin

6. anti-dote

7. none

8. pen-ta-gon

9. re-li-gion

10. semi-arid

11. im-be-cile

12. fin-ger

13. pic-ture

14. hexa-gon

15. step-father

16. kilo-meter

17. as is

18. gen-tili-ty

19. hemi-sphere

20. at-mos-phere

Review set 87

1. mental

2. moral

3. Parallelism

4. thermos

5. temperature

6. doesn't, any

7. is

8. was

9. us

10. he, we ("have" omitted)

11. sing, well

12. has, his/her

13. Those

14. flown

15. they

16. "Yes, Tom," replied his father, "this oven is self-cleaning. Ouch, it's hot!" (or Ouch! It's hot!)

17. (a) participle
    (b) verb
    (c) gerund

18. has been raising, present perfect progressive tense

19. true

20. (Unless) we can locate that woman with curlers in her hair

21. The Tower of London, a historic fortress in the city of London, was used as a royal residence and as a prison until Elizabethan times.

22. your

23. (a) adjective
    (b) adverb

24. clause

25. put, (is) putting, put, (has) put

26. most tentative

27. (a) allegories
    (b) bonuses
    (c) analogies

28. The Ladies of Avignon

29.

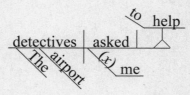

30.

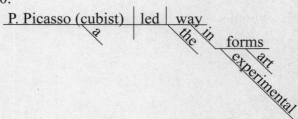

LESSON 88   Adverbs that Tell "When"

Practice 88

a. "Earlier" modifies "had been interested"

b. "later" modifies "rewarded"

c. "Yearly" modifies "visited"

d. "montly" modifies "met"

e.

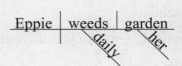

f.

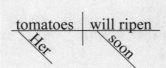

g. backup

h. Compression

i. peripherals

Review set 88

1. plot line

2. temperature

3. before

4. self-

5. Soliloquoy

6. well

7. he, her and me

8. our

9. me

10. aren't

11. doesn't, yours

12. whom

13. that

14. flew

15. less

16. Dear Sir Bevidere,
Please take me to the waterside and place me on the barge. I shll sail to the East, for there lies the Valley of Avalon. The current will carry me in an easterly direction.
Gratefully,
King Arthur

17. (a) verb
    (b) gerund
    (c) participle

18. Had chosen, past perfect tense

19. essential, essential

20. (After) the magmificent hall was completed

21. either, singular

22. my

23. (a) How? (*answer given*)
    (b) When?
    (c) Where?

24. to explain, adjective

25. stand, (is) standing, stood, (has) stood

26. he, Grandel

27. (a) no hyphen
    (b) as is
    (c) earth-worm

28. <u>National Geographic</u>

29.

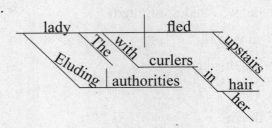

30.

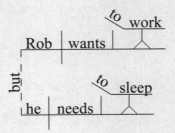

LESSON 89   **Adverbs that Tell "How Much"**

Practice 89

a. "Very" modifies the adjective "serious"

b. "rather" modifies the adverb "viciously"

c. "quite" modifies the predicate adjective "effective"

d. "absolutely" modifies the predicate adjective "crucial"

e. "n't" modifies the verb "did know"

f.

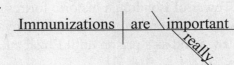

g.

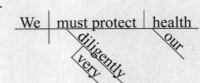

h. osteochondritis

i. osteo

j. osteoblasts

k. osteogenesis

l. osteoscope

Review set 89

1. temperature

2. Romance

3. symbol

4. physio-

5. natural

6. doesn't, any

7. Aren't

8. sits

9. We

10. she, I ("speak" omitted)

11. make, good

12. understand, their ("volunteers" can be counted)

13. saw, those

14. drew

15. me

16. On July 26, 2002, a class of geology students traveled to Tucson, Arizona, to photograph rock formations.

17. (a) participle
    (b) verb
    (c) gerund

18. have been examining, present perffect progressive tense

19. nonessential clause

20. (as) Grendel attacks their homeland

21. more persnickety

22. our

23. (a) peaceful, peacefully
    (b) harmful, harmfully

24. compound

25. sit, (is) sitting, sat, (has) sat

26. Frank Lloyd Wright, a famous American architect, designed houses to fit in with the features of the surrounding landscape.

27. (a) merry-go-rounds
    (b) glassfuls
    (c) children

28. Christina's World

29.

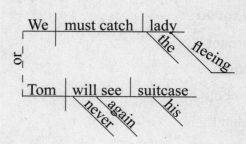

30.

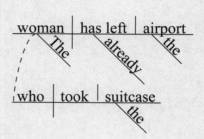

LESSON 90   **Comparison Adverbs**

Practice 90

a. shortest

b. more quickly

c. better

d. most appropriately

e. worse, worst

f. operating system

g. multitasking

h. application

More Practice 90

1. most gracefully

2. less

3. better

4. faster

5. longer

6. better

7. best

8. farther

9. less

10. most

Review set 90

1. narrator

2. mental

3. symbol

4. natural

5. peripheral

6. well

7. they

8. well equipped

9. well-equipped

10. our

11. doesn't, isn't, hers

12. who

13. which

14. beaten

15. highest

16. "Stop!" cried Mrs. Poovey to the taxi driver. "Please wait for me. I need to feed the cat, get my purse, and lock the door before I go."

17. "Having approached Hrothgar on friendly terms" modifies "Goths"

18. had sunk, past perfect tense, intransitive

19. simple sentence

20. run-on sentence

21. who

22. us

23. (a) truthful, truthfully
    (b) careful, carefully

24. to help, noun

25. write, (is) writing, wrote, (has) written

26. Everyone, singular

27. Word-of-mouth

28. <u>My Utmost for His Highest</u>

29.

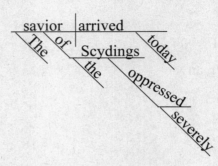

30.

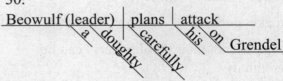

LESSON 91   The Semicolon • The Conjunctive Adverb

Practice 91

a. We . . . first: . . . second; . . . .

b. Khaki . . . acceptable; they are all part . . . .

c. The student . . . pants: therefore, she is . . . .

d. tri-

e. prototype

f. proto-

g. triarchy

h. deutero-

i. Deuteronomy

More Practice 91   *See Master Worksheets*

Review set 91

1. backup

2. compression

3. osteo-

4. measurement

5. Polychrome

6. aren't

7. could

8. makes

9. us

10. he, I ("learned" omitted)

11. Well

12. Good

13. promises, his/her

14. led

15. I

16. "Never mind," said Mrs. Poovey to the taxi driver. "You are in a hurry; therefore, I shall drive my own vehicle." (or) "You are in a hurry. Therefore, I shall . . . ."

17. mending the tent so well

18. will be receiving, future progressive tense, action

19. whenever I think of Denmark

20. phrase

21. essential part

22. and, but, or, for, nor, yet, so

23. better

24. Grover Cleveland, the twenty-second and twenty-fourth president of the United States, began his political career as Erie County sheriff in New York.

25. swing, (is) swinging, swung, (has) swung

26. (a) faithful, faithfully
    (b) joyful, joyfully

27. fast-growing, twenty-six

28. the, e

29.

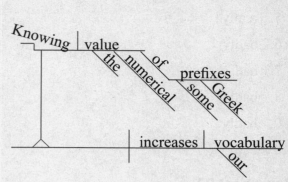

30.

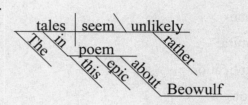

LESSON 92   Descriptive Adverbs • Adverb Usage

Practice 92

a. hexa-

b. tetragons

c. tetra-

d. pentad

e. penta-

f. hexapod

g. speedily, lazily, happily

h. carefully, fast, slowly, skillfully

i. surely

j. really

k. really

l. badly

m. badly

More Practice 92

1. surely

2. really

3. certainly

4. really

5. really

6. badly

7. bad

8. badly

9. badly

10. bad

Review set 92

1. bone-

2. natural

3. application

4. proto-

5. deutero-

6. she, themselves

7. ever, ridden, them

8. up-to-date

9. up to date

10. my

11. doesn't, aren't, ours

12. whom

13. well

14. flown

15. more

16. "Help!" screamed Mrs. Poovey to the police officer. "Can't you see that I need help? I didn't see the stop sign, so my car is wrecked."

17. to investigate, adjective

18. Will find, future tense, transitive

19. so that this computer file will use less space

20. (a) gerund
    (b) verb
    (c) participle

21. nonessential

22. we

23. best

24. compound

25. teach, (is) teaching, taught, (has) taught

26. nevertheless

27. Lorna baked my three favorite kinds of pie—fresh peach, banana cream, and French apple.

28. The Horse and his Boy

29.

neighbor (Mr. Poovey) | Has forgiven | wife
your / yet / his

30.

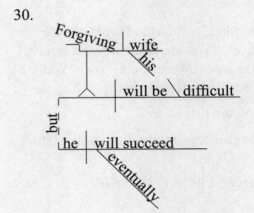

LESSON 93   The Colon

Practice 93

a. . . . 7:35 p.m. . . . .

b. . . . Proverbs 3:5–6.

c. . . . the following items: picture I.D., ...

d. Dear Assemblyman Mountjoy:

e. . . . these words: "The British . . . !"

f. octaroon

g. hepta

h. octo

i. ennead

j. ennea

k. heptose

Review set 93

1. bone
2. peripherals
3. earliest
4. deutero-
5. tri-
6. weren't, ever
7. Those, anything
8. feeds
9. we
10. they, I
11. adverb
12. really, well
13. has, his/her
14. striven
15. me
16. participle
17. gerund
18. "Whew!" exclaimed Mrs. Poovey to the driver whose car she had hit, "I did not injure you; however, I badly dented your car." (or) ". . . you. However, I . . . ."
19. phrase
20. seems, present tense, linking
21. (unless) Beowulf can destroy the dragon
22. either, singular
23. more carefully
24. think, (is) thinking, thought, (has) thought
25. run-on
26. on the other hand
27. (a) wouldn't
    (b) cobble-stone

28. Jenny will bring lettuce, tomatoes, and condiments; and Beth will bring meat, buns, and chips.

29.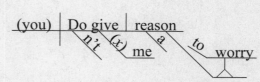

30.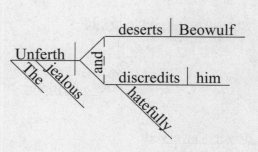

LESSON 94

The Prepositional Phrase as an Adverb • Diagramming

Practice 94

a. "like murderous barbarians" modifies "acted"
b. "in the 1830s" modifies "suppressed"
c. "in their riturals" modifies "sincere"
d. "into the hills" modifies "high"
e.

Spats | wandered
  far
  from
    home

f.

Nancy | found | him
  in
    meadow
    the

g. decades
h. ten
i. decathlon
j. deca (or deka)
k. decapod
l. dekameter

More Practice 94

1.

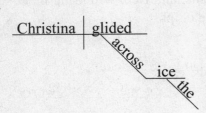

2.

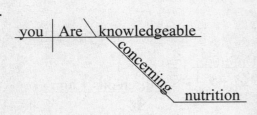

3.

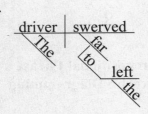

4. in the warm *rays,
   of the *sun

5. At the *shore,
   of the *Sea of Galilee,
   for *turtles and sand *fleas

Review set 94

1. three

2. second

3. tetra-

4. penta-

5. hexa-

6. he, really

7. ever, eaten

8. terror-stricken

9. terror stricken

10. my

11. doesn't, its

12. whom

13. really, well

14. slain

15. hardest

16. to fight, adjective

17. guten Morgen, gute Nacht

18. Dear King Beowulf,
    You defeated Grendel, so we have been
    spared much evil; nevertheless, the furious
    dragon is now ravaging our kingdom.
    With concern,
    Your loyal subjects
    (or) . . . much evil. Nevertheless, the
    furious . . . .

19. Will Beowulf and Wiglaf fight the dragon
    courageously?

20. has enclosed, present perfect tense,
    transitive

21. unless they strike down the foe

22. nonessential

23. him

24. buy, (is) buying, bought, (has) bought

25. compound

26. in addition

27. aban-don

28. Erika has purchased these items: sponges,
    soap, car wax, and tire cleaner.

29.

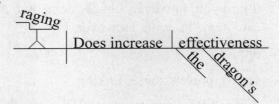

30.

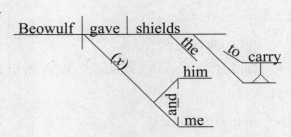

Practice 95

a. adverb

b. preposition

c. preposition

d. adverb

e. into

f. among

g. besides

h. download

i. Encryption

j. cache

Review set 95

1. hexapods

2. triarchy

3. hepta-

4. octo-

5. ennea-

6. is

7. are

8. Does

9. us

10. they, eat, we

11. infinitive

12. surely, well

13. proves

14. drawn

15. which

16. comes

17. <u>Cavia porcellus</u>

18. Dear Mrs. Poovey,
The auto body shop will charge me forty-five hundred dollars to repair my car.

Please write the check to Rondo's Auto Body before Monday, May 22.
Sincerely,
Tom Curtis

19. Duke Ellington, a great American composer, became the leader of a jazz band during the Roaring Twenties.

20. sentence fragment

21. (as) they desert the battlefield

22. essential

23. most carefully

24. sell, (is) selling, sold, (has) sold

25. one, singular

26. at the same time

27. The lady with the curlers—I don't know her name—was last seen in the airport parking lot.

28. The soil looks dry as a bone; the pansies have withered and died.

29.

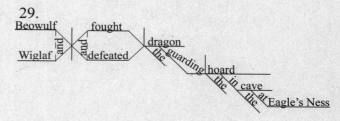

30.

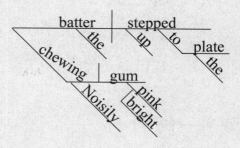

Practice 96

a. multi-

b. multiped

c. multivitamin

d. multiply

e. multitude

f. noun

g. adverb

h. adjective

i. to enter a tournament, enough

j. to watch the tournament, hopeful

k. To view the competitors, must arive

l.

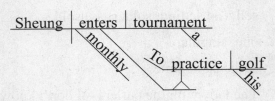

More Practice 96

1.

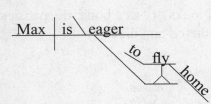

2.

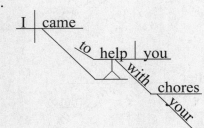

3.

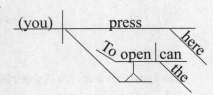

4.

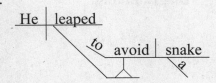

5.

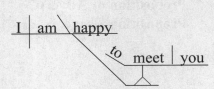

6.

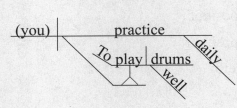

Review set 96

1. four

2. five

3. seven

4. ten

5. bones

6. her, really

7. doesn't, anybody

8. fast-moving

9. fast moving

10. our

11. There are, hers

12. who

13. surely, well

14. risen

15. farther

16. into, among

17. not, quite, very, rather, somewhat, too

18. "I will win the gold by my valor, or battle shall destroy me," Beowulf told his companions.
    Wiglaf reminded him, "You must defend yourself with all your might."

19. (a) busloads
    (b) geese
    (c) pocketknives

20. Has grown, present perfect tense, linking

21. simple

22. and, but, or, for, nor, yet, so

23. them

24. make, (is) making, made, (has) made

25. anti-dote

26. for this reason

27. <u>Superchief</u>

28. This book covers the eight parts of speech: adjectives, adverbs, conjunctions, interjections, nouns, prepositions, pronouns, and verbs.

29.

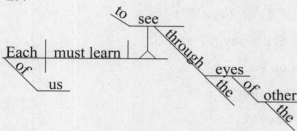

30.

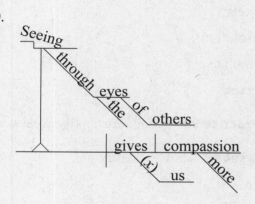

LESSON 97   The Apostrophe: Possessives

Practice 97

a. ambivalent

b. ambi-

c. ambiversion

d. ambidextrous

e. ambisinister

f. ambilateral

g. brothers-in-law's

h. Denny, Daisy, and Donny's

i. geese's

j. duck's

k. lice's

l. Hoss's

More Practice 97

1. parable's

2. consul's

3. louse's

4. statue's

5. ally's

6. hypocrite's

7. machinist's

8. platoon's

9. moose's

10. ants'

11. caterpillars'

12. criteria's

13. caddies'

14. children's

15. women's

16. syllabi's

Review set 97

1. nine

2. ten

3. ten

4. encryption

5. download

6. anything

7. pays

8. Isn't

9. We

10. we, sleep, they

11. adverb

12. surely

13. diagrams, well

14. lay

15. that

16. bolt

17. here, still, almost, now, quite

18. Dear Tom Curtis,
    Enclosed is a check for twenty-three hundred dollars to cover the cost of repairs on your car. I will send you the remaining twenty-two hundred when I return from Heidelberg, Germany, on April 1, 2017.
    Sincerely,
    Mrs. Poovey

19. to tell a lie, adverb

20. has been perpetuating, past perfect progressive tense, transitive

21. (Whatever) Kilhuch desires

22. essential clause

23. anyone, singular

24. hold, (is) holding, hald, (has) held

25. more (or less) gently

26. consequently

27. Beowulf's faithful followers traveled to view the wonders of Eagle's Ness—the strange creature, the doughty king, the flagons, and the swords.

28. Wiglaf was indefatigable; moreover, he encouraged Beofulf to remain strong to the end.

29.

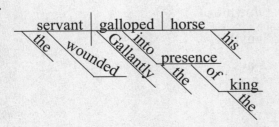

30.

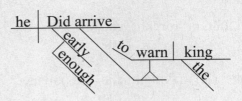

LESSON 98   **The Apostrophe: Contractions, Omitting Digits and Letters**

Practice 98

a. Aren't

b. '02

c. I'll, 'o, it's, it'll, what's

d. She's, sayin', isn't

e. *ah's*

f. wouldn't

g. they're

h. pixels

i. resolution

j. template

k. server

More Practice 98   *See Master Worksheets*

Review set 98

1. ten

2. cache

3. many

4. stereotype

5. skin

6. he, really

7. adverb

8. full-time

9. full time

10. our

11. theirs, anywhere

12. whom, doesn't

13. Badly

14. flew

15. most

16. besides, between

17. (a) The Curtises'
    (b) Jenny's
    (c) mother-in-law's

18. "I need your help, for my suitcase is still missing," said Tom to Detective Onsworth. "A woman with curlers in her hair took it, but I don't know this woman's identity."

19. At my mother's school in Detroit, Michigan, SIster Mary taught the following subjects: mathematics, music, Latin, and history.

20. John Dalton, an English schoolteacher in the early 1800s, proposed the idea that all mater is composed of atoms.

21. compound sentence

22. (If) Samson has a haircut

23. she

24. Kilhuch

25. phrase

26. hexa-pod

27. nevertheless

28. Lady Guinevere

29.

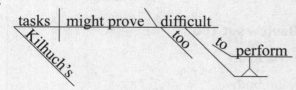

30.

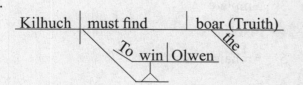

Practice 99

a. soliloquy

b. soli-

c. solo

d. solitaire

e. solitude

f. noun clause

g. adjective clause

h. ~~noun~~ adj. clause

i. adverb clause

j. noun clause

Review set 99

1. many

2. both

3. bone

4. application

5. both

6. anywhere

7. like

8. is

9. those

10. We, they ("have had" omitted)

11. transitive

12. really

13. carries, his

14. striven

15. which

16. comes

17. (a) brothers-in-law's
    (b) James's
    (c) The Rivases'

18. After reading Mrs. Poovey's letter, Tom shouted, "Dadgummit, I cannot wait until April 1, 2017, to repair my car! Is this lady crazy?" (or) . . . "Dadgummit! I . . . ."

19. Olwen will become Kilhuch's bride, and they'll live happily ever after.

20. most (or least) loudly

21. No one, singular

22. while he was setting up the office computer network

23. and, but, or, for, nor, yet, so

24. wake, (is) waking, woke, or waked, (has) waked

25. "drinking his tea" modifies "man"

26. deka-meter

27. hence

28. has proven, present perfect tense, linking

29.

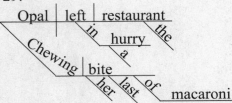
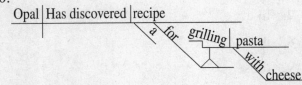

30.

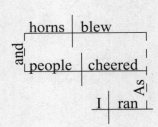

The Complex Sentence • The Compound-Complex Sentence • Diagramming the Adverb Clause

Practice 100

a. simple

b. complex

c. compound-complex

d.

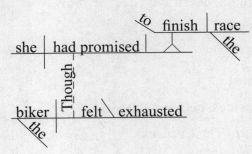

e. circumvent

f. circumnavigate

g. circumference

h. circum-

i. circumspect

More Practice 100

1. complex

2. compound

3. simple

4. compound-complex

5. complex

6.

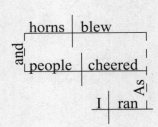

Additional Diagramming Practice

See Master Worksheets

Review set 100

1. many

2. both

3. template

4. Pixels

5. Archaic

6. he

7. really well

8. sun-bleached

9. exclamatory

10. John's

11. a, himself

12. who, doesn't

13. that

14. shone

15. better

16. between

17. (a) fox's
    (b) foxes'
    (c) Charles Dickens's

18. I. The case of the missing suitcase
    A. Clues
    B. Suspects
    C. Evidence

19. Detective Onsworth must consider the evidence; moreover, he must question all the suspects.

20. more (or less) loudly

21. nonessential

22. (Although) those elderly men look pitiful and ragged

23. I

24. simple sentence

25. noun clause

26. exempli gratia

27. for example

28. has been envying, present perfect progressive tense, transitive

29.

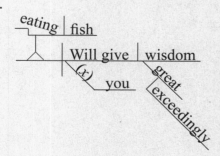

30.

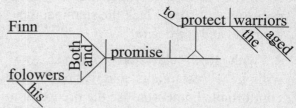

LESSON 101   Parallel Structure

Practice 101

a. B

b. A

c. B

d. For . . . <u>a</u> fish, <u>a</u> horned toad, and <u>a</u> rabbit. (or) For . . . <u>a</u> fish, horned toad, and rabbit.

e. In his . . . against dragons, against thieves, and against monsters. (or) In his . . . against dragons, thieves, and monsters.

f. parallel

g. paradigm

h. paragon

i. para-

j. parasitess

k. parallel

More Practice 101

1. Stephen stuck sticky notes around his desk, inside his books, and <u>on</u> his computer.

2. He will stick notes either outside the door or <u>inside</u> the house.

3. John has neither the patience nor <u>the time</u> to repair the computer.

4. Elspeth studied her Spanish, called her friend, and <u>fed</u> her fish.

5. This afternoon, she will begin shopping, cleaning, and <u>planning</u> for the party.

6. My cousin has the strength of an ox, the speed of a cheetah, and <u>the wisdom of</u> an owl.

7. I lack the stamina, courage, and desire . . . . (or) I lack the stamina, the courage, and the desire . . . .

8. . . . without . . . television programs, without . . . restaurants, and without her comfortable home. (or, use the preposition only with the first part.)

9. In her free time, she liks to read mystery novels, to draw anteaters, and to work crossword puzzles.

10. Debby bought not only a cherry pie but also a banana cream pie.

Review set 101

1. ambivalent
2. resolution
3. pixels
4. soli-
5. alone
6. doesn't, any
7. eats
8. are
9. those
10. us
11. intransitive
12. surely
13. has, his
14. shone
15. that
16. scamper
17. (a) commander-in-chief's
    (b) gentlemen's
    (c) actress's
18. Finn searched for Saba, his true love, in remote glens, dark forests, and deep chasms.
19. Dear Saba,
    I'm thankful that my two hounds, Bran and

Sceolaun, found you. You're one of the fairest maidens I've ever seen. Would you consider being my wife?
All my love,
Finn

20. multi-tude
21. their, Finn and Oisin
22. beat, (is) beating, beat, (has) beaten
23. either/or, neither/nor, not only/but also, both/and
24. complex sentence
25. adjective clause
26. Wearing the garb of a queen, maiden
27. however
28. has observed, present perfect tense, action

29.

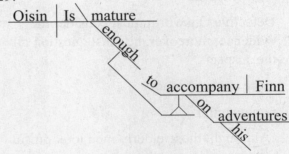

30.

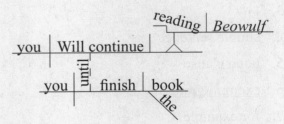

LESSON 102   Active or Passive Voice

Practice 102

a. passive
b. active
c. passive
d. active

e. upload

f. firewall

g. webmaster

h. spam

More Practice 102

1. passive

2. active

3. active

4. passive

5. passive

6. active

7. passive

8. active

Review set 102

1. one

2. around

3. around

4. both

5. one

6. she

7. surely, well

8. complex

9. subordinate

10. anything

11. our

12. whom

13. coordinating conjunction

14. harder

15. shined

16. among

17. (a) steeds'
    (b) maidens'
    (c) youths'

18. Dear Mrs. Poovey,
    If you wish to settle this case out of court, please contact my personal attorney, Mr. Chatwell, at the following address: 42 Leisurely Lane, Anaconda, Texas.
    Sincerely,
    Tom Curtis

19. Turbo's faher, Stanley, has fleas, ticks, and mange; but his mother, Sasha, does not.

20. (a) sovereignties
    (b) Joneses
    (c) bays

21. nonessential part

22. most imaginatively

23. me

24. simple sentence

25. (as soon as) you have bathed them, adverb clause

26. The Odyssey of Homer

27. consequently

28. Allison likes to ride bikes, swim laps, and play basketball.

29.

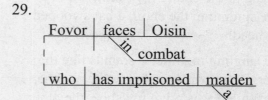

30.

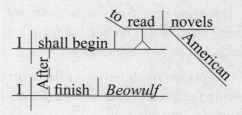

LESSON 103   Dangling or Misplaced Modifiers

Practice 103

a. B

b. A

c. B

d. B

e. audiologist

f. audi-

g. Auditions

h. audience

i. audible

More Practice 103

1. (1) Dangling modifier—sounds like Harriet's book was rushing to class. (2) While Harriet was rushing to class, her book fell out of her backpack.

2. (1) Misplaced modifier—sounds like the writer had been written and revised. (2) I was ready to publish the paper that had been written and revised.

3. (1) Misplaced prepositional phrase— Sounds like the bull was on its way to the hotel! (2) On the way to our hotel, we saw a huge bull.

4. (1) Dangling modifier—was the bat singing in the choir? (2) While we were singing in the choir, a bat swooped overhead.

5. (1) Dangling modifier—sounds like the other player was tying the writer's shoe. (2) While I was tying my shoe, the other player made a point against our team.

6. (1) Dangling modifier—were the pews leaving church? (2) While we were leaving church, the pews were empty.

7. (1) Misplaced modifier—was the sparrow mowing the lawn? (2) Mowing the lawn, he found a litle sparrow.

8. (1) Dangling modifier—was the phone rushing to get ready for school? (2) While I was rushing to get ready for school, the phone rang.

9. (1) Misplaced modifier—sounds like Josh is completely untamed! (2) Josh suggested we stay away from his python since it is completely untamed.

10. (1) Misplaced prepositional phrase, "after class." Does it tell when Jared wanted to know, or when the teacher said something to his friend? (2) Place "after class" either at the beginning or at the end of the sentence.

11. (1) Dangling modifier—sounds like two ants were making a sandwich! (2) While I was making a sandwich, two ants crawled out of the bread bag.

12. (1) Misplaced modifier—sounds like the writer was beating on the roof steadily. (2) I could hardly wait till the rain stopped because it was beating on the roof steadily.

Review set 103

1. around

2. circumspect

3. beside

4. Parallel

5. parasite

6. aren't, any

7. remains

8. she ("has" omitted)

9. hand-stitched

10. We

11. compound-complex

12. really

13. live

14. risen

15. which

16. jumps

17. (a) Sherry's
    (b) The Gregorys'
    (c) Mr. Cruz's

18. Dr. Yokoi, I believe, will offer her seminar on figurative language in epic literature on Friday, October 12, at 10 a.m.

19. "Let's go!" Mrs. Poovey shouted to her husband. "I don't want to miss my flight." "Must you always go out in public wearing curlers in your hair?" asked Mr. Poovey.

20. lead, (is) leading, led, (has) led

21. Alfred Lord Tennyson, a great English poet during the Victorian age, wrote a series of twelve stories, called *Idylls of the King*, about King Arthur and his knights.

22. para-digm

23. him—Oisin; his—Oisin

24. compound sentence

25. that you might move away, adjective

26. passive voice

27. moreover

28. The job includes preparing the surface, taping the edges, and painting the top.

29.

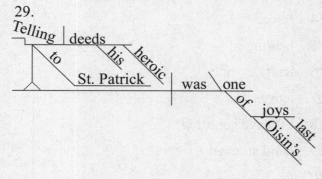

30.

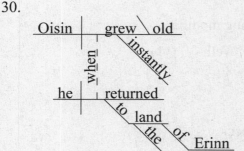

Practice 104

a. . . . "She [Anne Frank] was . . . ."

b. . . . twelve thousand dollars ($12,000).

c. . . . (a book to read or a toy) . . . .

d. . . . (wow!) . . . .

e. commingle

f. correlate

g. coadjutor

h. convene

i. collateral

Review set 104

1. paragon

2. paradigm

3. upload

4. Spam

5. webmaster

6. him

7. really, well

8. active

9. passive

10. anything

11. my

12. who

13. intransitive

14. hardest

15. shone

16. among

17. (a) Mrs. Campos's
    (b) The Camposes'
    (c) Saturday's

18. Marco comforted the anxious Guatemalan family with the following words: Jamás duerme el que te cuida.

19. "I wear curlers to style my hair, and I don't care what others think," declared Mrs. Poovey.

20. (a) Thomases
    (b) liberties
    (c) ladies-in-waiting

21. B

22. more (or less) clearly

23. our

24. complex sentence

25. (as) Chuchulain skillfully drove the horses and chariot, adverb clause

26. active voice

27. on the other hand

28. He said he would need a horse, a chariot, and a rider

29.
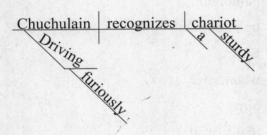

30.
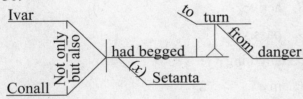

LESSON 105

Interjections

Practice 105

a. Ah

b. Bam!

c. Hey

d. Cool!

e.
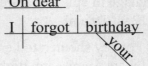
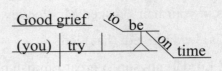

f.

g. contraband

h. contradict

i. contralateral

j. contrast

k. contra

l. contravene

Review set 105

1. firewall

2. audi-

3. Archaic

4. farce

5. hearing

6. isn't, anyone

7. leaves, his

8. I ("have" omitted)

9. hand stitched

10. us

11. dangling modifier

12. surely, well

13. wakes

14. that

15. between

16. has been making, present perfect progressive tense

17. (a) chariot's
    (b) Fergus's
    (c) horses'

18. According to <u>Monrovia Music</u>, the police apprehended Mrs. Poovey as a suspect in the suitcase theft, but she is out on ten thousand dollars ($10,000) bail.

19. "I think," said Mr. Poovey to his wife, "that your hair curlers attracted the attention of the authorities."

20. Kitty Hawk, North Carolina, the site of Orville and Wilbur Wright's first airplane flight, is now a national historical monument.

21. B

22. essential (no commas—Debby has more than one dog.)

23. rise, (is) rising, rose, (has) risen

24. simple sentence

25. (that) my fencing opponent was ambidextrous, noun clause

26. Chuchulain drove the chariot.

27. Only a few Egyptian papyrus rolls have survived; (however), scholars can learn much from them.

28. The Hittites conquered Anatolia (Turkey), forced out foreign traders, and took over the metal trade.

29.

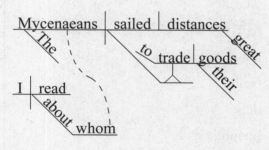

30.

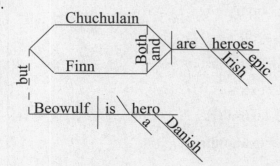

Practice 106

a. tres(t)le

b. (w)hom

c. (g)nu

d. (k)now

e. (k)nit

f. (k)nelt

g. (G)nostic

h. (w)rangler

i. disarray

j. dis-

k. disbelief

l. dishearten

m. disown

n. disappoint

Review set 106

1. heard
2. hearing
3. sound
4. around
5. together
6. he
7. surely
8. phrase
9. Besides
10. any
11. Oisin's
12. who
13. transitive
14. earlier
15. any, between

16. Has insulted, present perfect tense, transitive

17. (a) Jerry and Iris's
    (b) materials'
    (c) Egyptians'

18. Dear Mother,
    I am asking you and my wife to love one another for my sake. The king has ordered me to go into the royal service, so you must take care of each other.
    Love,
    Cid

19. Some of the Egyptian gods and goddesses had these names: Hathor, Taweret, Ptuh, Apis, and Thoth.

20. (a) Gomezes
    (b) Henrys
    (c) parentheses

21. B

22. most (or least) clearly

23. its

24. compound sentence

25. (As) they studied the stars and planets, adverb

26. Cid gave the leper food and shelter

27.
    Cid had conquered five Moorish kings; (nevertheless,) he sent them back to their own country without a ransom

28. I am thankful for family, shelter, and food.
    (or) I am thankful for family, for shelter, and for food.

29.
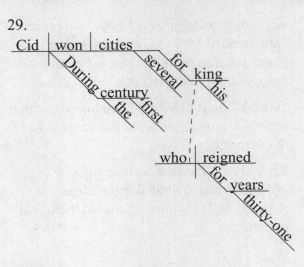

30.
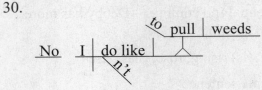

LESSON 107   **Spelling Rules: Silent Letters**
             p, b, l, u, h, n, and *gh*

Practice 107

a. g**u**arantee

b. thorou**gh**

c. c**h**arisma

d. r**h**inoceros

e. wou**l**d

f. ha**l**f

g. a**l**ms

h. cau**l**k

i. de**b**t

j. **p**neumatic

k. bom**b**

l. yo**l**k

m. extrasensory

n. extra-

o. extrovert

p. extraordinary

q. extracurricular

r. extrospection

Review set 107

1. together
2. with
3. against
4. together
5. oppose
6. any
7. has, her/his
8. they
9. self-reliant
10. We
11. phrase
12. well
13. after
14. between
15. Rodrigo (also called Cid, Chief, and the Perfect One) had a successful and happy life.
16. (a) whistle
    (b) badge
    (c) knowledge
17. (a) lass's
    (b) Cid and the leper's
    (c) garments'
18. In May, 2002, <u>Luxuriant Landscaping</u> magazine featured an article titled "Propagating Perennials for Pennies."
19. There is, in fact, a story explaining God's protection over Cid as he traveled to Compostella to pay homage to Saint Mary on January 12, 1026.
20. John Keats, a gifted 19th-century Romantic poet, was the son of a livery stable owner in London
21. B

22. essential part (I have other friends besides Debby—no commas)
23. raise, (is) raising, raised, (has) raised
24. complex
25. (where) I was going, noun clause
26. Uncle Richard drove Miss Petunia Schnootz to the bus station.
27. Mrs. Poovey will write Tom a letter of apology; (in addition), she will pay for his car repairs.
28. You may use that new computer for playing games, for communicating with your friends, and for writing your papers.
29.

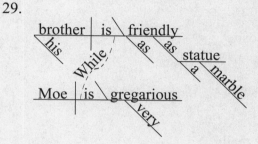

30.

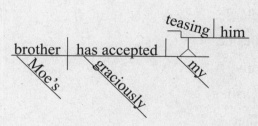

LESSON 108   **Spelling Rules: Suffixes, Part 1**

Practice 108

a. blameless
b. drowsiness
c. weariest
d. steadily
e. forceful
f. slaving
g. lately
h. tamer

i. famous

j. rating

k. plentiful

l. inter-

m. interscholastic

n. interfere

o. intercept

p. intervene

q. intervene

Review set 108

1. against

2. contra

3. opposite

4. lack

5. romance

6. her

7. she, really

8. clause

9. beside

10. any

11. Oisin's

12. that

13. forsaken

14. earliest

15. Mrs. Poovey still owes Tom a hundred dollars ($100) and a suitcase full of gummy candy.

16. (a) lam(b)
    (b) (g)nash
    (c) (p)sal(m)

17. (a) charters'
    (b) geese's
    (c) cattle's

18. Buon compleanno, an Italian birthday greeting, appeared on the card that came with my roses.

19. Alvar Fanez said, "Yes, I am forced to be content with only partial pardon for Cid."

20. (a) gentlemen
    (b) octopuses, octopi
    (c) flies

21. B

22. more (or less) reluctantly

23. their

24. compound-complex

25. (When) the bear cub saw us, adverb clause

26. Miss Petunia Schnootz had driven Uncle Richard crazy.

27. You should buy me lunch because we're friends; (besides), it's my birthday.

28. In case of invasion, Cid stored provisions, strengthened walls, and **armed** the citizens.

29.

30.

LESSON 109   Spelling Rules: Suffixes, Part 2

Practice 109

a. chipped

b. flopping

c. badly

d. eyeful

e. sadness

f.   trans-

g.   trasnfixed

h.   transcontinental

i.   transcended

j.   transmit

Review set 109

1.   dis-

2.   outside of

3.   beyond

4.   outgoing

5.   between

6.   anyone

7.   gives, his/her

8.   she

9.   fast-moving

10.   us

11.   brackets

12.   well

13.   really

14.   among

15.   (a)   flaming
      (b)   blameless
      (c)   modified

16.   (a)   knuckle
      (b)   sleigh
      (c)   batch

17.   (a)   Mr. Jone's
      (b)   The Joneses'
      (c)   Debby's

18.   Didelphis virginiana is the scientific name for opossum, a nocturnal mammal that often lives in trees.

19.   "The Infantes of Carrion" is tht title of the characters of Diego and Ferrando.

20.   Ferrando and Diego, the future sons-in-law of Cid, behave selfishly and pathetically.

21.   A

22.   nonessential part

23.   hang, (is) hanging, hung, (has) hung

24.   simple sentence

25.   (that) dangled above me, adjective clause

26.   A pet lion frightened Diego and Ferrando

27.   Those observing the cowardly behavior of Ferrando and Diego began laughing and making fun of the brothers; (however,) Diego and Ferrando failed to see the humor in the situation.

28.   Tortoises don't like swimming, surfing, or water skiing.

29.

30.

LESSON
110

Spelling Rules: *ie* or *ei*

Practice 110

a.   niece

b.   seize (exception)

c.   reprieve

d.   receipt

e.   weight

f.   sleigh

g.   omni-

h.   omnipotent

i. omnivorous

j. omnifarious

k. omniscient

Review set 110

1. beyond

2. between

3. across

4. all

5. across

6. them

7. they, really

8. phrase

9. fast moving

10. any

11. those

12. which

13. striven

14. more

15. receive

16.   a. g(u)arantee
      b. plum(b)er
      c. yo(l)k

17.   a. bees'
      b. fleas'
      c. oxen's

18. Jack London's most famous novel, <u>The Call of the Wild</u>, was published in 1903.

19. On January 4, 1076, an all-knowing sage confronted a self-righteous hypocrite; moreover, the sage exposed the hypocrite to public scrutiny. (or) . . . hypocrite. Moreover, . . .

20.   a. suffixes
      b. morning glories
      c. Dennises

21.   a. shopping
      b. madly
      c. strapped

22. most (or least) reluctantly

23. them

24. compound sentence

25. (that) his future sons-in-law were proud and scornful—adjective clause

26. Jenny and her father painted that entire two-story house.

27. false

28. B

29.

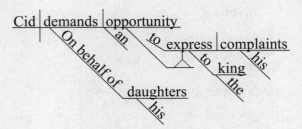

30.

For 1–4, tell whether the sentence is declarative, interrogative, exclamatory, or imperative.

1. Fables were passed down by word of mouth. __declarative__
(1)

2. Do you think that Aesop was creative? __interrogative__
(1)

3. Read as much as you can. __imperative__
(1)

4. Watch out! __exclamatory__
(1)

5. Circle each letter that should be capitalized in this sentence: On (w)ednesday, (m)r. (w)u will plant an
(5) (a)ustralian willow at (s)anta (a)nita (p)ark in (c)alifornia.

In the space to the right, diagram the simple subject and simple predicate of sentences 6 and 7.

6. Did you understand the instructions?   you | Did understand
(2, 4)

7. The country mouse loved his home.   mouse | loved
(2, 4)

For 8–10, circle the best word to complete each sentence.

8. Does the country mouse (adopt, adept, (adapt)) well to the city?
(1)

9. *Humane* means (ape-like, (kind,) cruel).
(3)

10. The American flag (waives, (waves)) from many homes.
(5)

For 11–13, write whether the expression is a sentence fragment, run-on sentence, or complete sentence:

11. A camel dances like a monkey it looks ridiculous. __run-on sentence__
(3)

12. The farmer and his wife prove their impulsiveness. __complete sentence__
(3)

13. Killing the goose, the source of the golden eggs. __sentence fragment__
(3)

Make a complete sentence from fragments 14 and 15.

14. Has no brains. __A mask has no brains. Answers will vary.__
(3)

15. A fox with a bad attitude. __A fox with a bad attitude complains. Answers will vary.__
(3)

For 16 and 17, add periods and capital letters to correct the run-on sentences.

16. The fox had a bad attitude. **H**e said that the grapes were probably sour.
(3, 5)

17. The gnat made a fool of himself. **H**e thought that he was more important than he really was.
(3, 5)

For sentences 18 and 19, circle the action verb.

18. The farmer and his wife (slaughtered) the goose.
(4)

19. A hawk (captured) the mouse and the frog.
(4)

Answers will vary.
detests, abhors, hates
20. Replace the verb in the sentence below with one that might be more precise. loathes, despises
(4)

The city mouse dislikes the country.

1. In the sentence below, circle each noun and label it *S* for singular or *P* for plural.
(9)

(Monkeys) laughed at the dancing (camel.)
     P   **S**

2. In the sentence below, circle each noun and label it *F* for feminine, *M* for masculine, *I* for indefinite, or *N*
(9) for neuter.
         I   **F**   **M**   **N**
Like my (dog), that (doe) and that (buck) have beautiful brown (eyes.)

3. Circle the compound noun in this sentence: The (soapbox) derby is next Saturday, February 3.
(9)

4. Circle the possessive noun in this sentence: The basketball (player's) shoes provided good traction.
(9)

5. Circle the correct verb form for this sentence: She researched the topic and (types, (typed)) her report.
(6)

6. Replace the blank with the singular present tense form of the verb: Many people <u>floss</u> their teeth daily,
(6) but Ross ____<u>flosses</u>____ his teeth twice each day.

7. In the sentence below, circle the verb phrase and label it past, present, or future tense.
(6, 10)

Nancy and Jim (will adopt) a border collie. ____<u>future</u>____ tense

8. Circle each helping verb from this list: his (am) car (was) (were) tea (being) (been) pay fight
(8)
rust tan (could) (should) (would) (has) (have) mad to (does) (did) (shall) fill

In the space to the right, diagram the simple subject and simple predicate of sentences 9 and 10.

9. The police will record your account of the incident.   <u>police</u> | <u>will record</u>
(2, 4)

10. Set your umbrella on the floor.   <u>(you)</u> | <u>set</u>
(2, 4)

For 11–13, write whether the expression is a complete sentence, sentence fragment, or run-on sentence.

11. We thought we had missed the bus then it appeared. <u>run-on sentence</u>
(3)

12. With wisdom and stamina far greater than mine. <u>sentence fragment</u>
(3)

13. Approaching American literature with an open mind, we can appreciate its authors. <u>complete sentence</u>
(3)

14. Circle the abstract noun from this sentence: Three men survived the fiery furnace, for they had (faith.)
(7)

15. Circle the collective noun in this sentence: A (herd) of cattle grazed in the meadow.
(7)

16. Unscramble these words to make an interrogative sentence.
(1)

you   what   about   do   know   Babylon
<u>What do you know about Babylon?</u>

17. Circle each letter that should be capitalized in this sentence: After the bombing of (p)earl (h)arbor, the (u)nited
(5) (s)tates became an ally of (g)reat (b)ritain and (f)rance in (w)orld (w)ar II.

Circle the best word to complete sentences 18–20.

18. A microbus is a (large, (small), heavy) bus.
(4)

19. The prefix (macro-, micro-, (miso-)) means hatred.
(7)

20. My good friend is also my (alley, (ally)).
(8)

1. For a–d, circle the correct verb form.
(14)

    (a) You (am, (are), is)   (b) They (am, (are), is)   (c) It (do, (does))   (d) I ((do), does)

For 2–5, write the plural of each singular noun.

2. library ___libraries___
(12, 13)

3. alley ___alleys___
(12, 13)

4. glass ___glasses___
(12, 13)

5. fistful ___fistfuls___
(12, 13)

For sentences 8–10, circle the entire verb phrase and name its tense "past," "present," or "future."

8. During frontier days, people (concocted) tall tales about heroic cowboys. ___past___ tense
(6, 10)

9. One of eighteen children, a baby, (falls) out the back of a covered wagon. ___present___ tense
(6, 10)

10. A mother coyote (will raise) this baby. ___future___ tense
(6, 10)

11. Circle each helping verb in this sentence:
(8)

    Coyotes (might have) taught Pecos Bill the secrets of survival on the prairie.

12. Underline each noun in this sentence and circle the one that is compound:
(9)

    While playing on the <u>prairie</u> with the <u>antelope</u> and <u>rabbits</u>, <u>Bill</u> meets a <u>man</u> on (<u>horseback</u>)

13. Circle each abstract noun from this list: rattlesnake   (imagination)   cowboy   (confidence)
(7)

14. Write the present participle, past tense, and past participle of the verb *howl*.
(15)

    _____ (is) howling, howled, (has) howled _____

Circle the correct word to complete sentences 15–17.

15. This sentence is (declarative, imperative, (interrogative), exclamatory): Was Pecos Bill a real person?
(1)

16. Although he thought he was a coyote, Pecos Bill was actually ((human), humane).
(3)

17. The Greek prefix (micro-, miso-, (macro-)) means large.
(2)

18. Circle the complete sentence from the word groups below.
(3)

    During a long, hot drought in the state of Texas.

    Jumping on his horse, Widow-Maker, and riding to Oklahoma.

    (Pecos Bill lassoes a cyclone.)

19. Circle each letter that should be capitalized in the sentence below.
(5, 11)

    (y)es, (i) believe he will bring rain back to (t)exas before (s)eptember.

20. Diagram the simple subject and simple predicate of this sentence:
(2, 4)

    Pecos Bill might have howled like a coyote.

          <u>Pecos Bill</u> | <u>might have howled</u>

Circle the correct word to complete sentences 1–5.

1. Paul Bunyan was tall in (statue, (stature), statute).
(10)

2. The Greek root *mania* means (large, hatred, (passion)) or madness.
(16)

3. American tall tales (am, is, (are)) full of humorous exaggerations.
(14)

4. The tall tale hero Paul Bunyan (have, (has)) a blue ox named Babe.
(14)

5. (Do, (Does)) Paul really create earthquakes with his hiccups?
(14)

For sentences 6–8, underline the entire verb phrase and complete the name of its tense by adding "present," "past," or "future."

6. Has the logger actually blown birds from Maine to California with his sneeze? ___present___ perfect
(18) tense

7. According to the tale, the giant baby ox had been shivering in a snowdrift. ___past___ perfect
(18) progressive tense

8. By the end of the story, Paul will have dug the entire Mississippi River with his shovel. ___future___
(18) perfect tense

9. Underline each noun in this sentence and circle the one that is collective: My (family) believes that Paul
(7) Bunyan cut out the Grand Canyon with his ax.

10. Circle each abstract noun in this list: snow (exaggeration) canal (humor) Alaska (heresy)
(7)

11. Circle each possessive noun from this list: Babes (Babe's) countries, (country's) loggers, (loggers')
(9)

For 12 and 13, write the plural of each noun.

12. batch ___batches___   **13.** penny ___pennies___
(12, 13)   (12, 13)

14. Write the present participle, past tense, and past participle of the verb *exaggerate*.
(15)

(is) exaggerating, exaggerated, (has) exaggerated

15. Circle the gerund in this sentence: Paul Bunyan's fantastic (logging) provided lumber for homes, schools,
(19) churches, boats, and furniture.

Circle each preposition in sentences 16 and 17.

16. (According to) the tale, Paul pulled the half-frozen baby ox (from under) the blue snowdrift and warmed it
(16, 17) (in front of) the fire.

17. (On account of) this amazing strength, this hero could cut a hundred trees (with) one swing (of) his ax.
(16, 17)

18. Circle each letter that should be capitalized in this sentence: (i)f you visit the state of (a)laska, you might
(5, 20) still hear the echoes when (p)aul (b)unyan shouts, "(t)imber!"

In the space to the right, diagram the simple subject and simple predicate of sentences 19 and 20.

19. Blue's shivering had attracted Paul's attention.
(4, 19)

20. Was the snow shivering also?   snow | Was shivering
(2, 4)

shivering
had attracted

Circle the best word(s) to complete sentences 1–6.

1. The mother duck will (sit, set, sat) on the largest egg until it hatches.
(24,)

2. The largest egg (lay, laid, lied) in the nest after all the others had hatched.
(23)

3. That little duck (have, has) finally broken out of the shell.
(14)

4. (Do, Does) he look like the other ducklings?
(14)

5. This sentence is (declarative, interrogative, imperative, exclamatory): Look! That's life!
(1)

6. The following is a (sentence fragment, run-on sentence, complete sentence): The ugly, gray duckling swam.
(3)

For 7 and 8, write the plural form of each singular noun.

7. Jenny ___Jennys___   **8.** woman ___women___
(9)   (12, 13)

9. Circle each letter that should be capitalized in this sentence: in hans christian andersen's "the ugly
(5, 20) duckling," a little duck says, "i am so ugly that the dog won't even bite me!"

10. Circle each preposition from this sentence: The ugly, gray duckling swam around the pond, behind the
(16, 17) mother duck, alongside of the other ducklings.

For sentences 11–14, underline the entire verb phrase and complete the name of its tense by adding "past," "present," or "future."

11. The ugly duckling <u>has developed</u> a complex about his appearance. ___present___ perfect tense
(18)

12. By the end of the fairy tale, he <u>will have transformed</u> into a beautiful swan. ___future___ perfect
(18) tense

13. He <u>will be rejoicing</u> after the hard winter. ___future___ progressive tense
(21)

14. In the spring, the duckling <u>had been traveling</u> for many miles. ___past___ perfect progressive
(21) tense

15. From the sentence below, underline each concrete noun and circle the one that is abstract.
(7)
           The ugly <u>duckling</u> suffered persecution from the other <u>ducks</u> in the <u>pond</u>.

16. Circle the gerund in this sentence: Flapping its wings brought freedom to the ugly duckling.
(19)

17. Circle the infinitive in this sentence: To persecute the less fortunate seems cruel.
(23)

For 18 and 19, circle to indicate whether the expression is a phrase or a clause.

18. from a clumsy, dark-gray bird to a beautiful swan   (phrase, clause)
(24)

19. before the duckling discovered his transformation   (phrase, clause)
(24)

20. In the space to the right, diagram the simple
(23, 25) subject, simple predicate, and direct object of this
           sentence: The swan has been learning to fly.

```
                                              to \ fly
                                                  \
                          swan | has been learning | \
```

Circle the best word(s) to complete sentences 1–9.

1. The Greek prefix *megalo-* means (madness, small, (large)).
(17)

2. Did (there, (their), they're) dog bark all night?
(19)

3. The (progressive, (perfect)) verb tense shows action that has been completed.
(18, 21)

4. The most commonly used adjectives, and the shortest, are the ((articles), pronouns) *a, an,* and *the.*
(28)

5. Examples of ((possessive), descriptive) adjectives are *his, her, their, your, its, our,* and *my.*
(28)

6. The sentence below is (declarative, imperative, interrogative, (exclamatory)):
(1)

     Hey, my sweet peas have disappeared!

7. The word group below is a ((sentence fragment), run-on sentence, complete sentence):
(3)

     A large, well-kept garden on the outskirts of the city.

8. This word group is a (phrase, (clause)): when summer comes again
(24)

9. The sentence below contains an (action, (linking)) verb.
(4, 22)

     The rabbit felt fearful of my basset hound, Max.

For 10 and 11, write the plural form of each noun.

10. wife ___wives___   **11.** party ___parties___
(12, 13)   (12, 13)

For 12 and 13, circle each letter that should be capitalized.

12. (t)he gardener explained, "(i) have been chasing that rabbit all over (f)lora (s)treet."
(5, 20)

13. (d)ear professor (h)atti,
(5, 29)

     (t)here are many different religions in the (w)est....

          (s)incerely,

          (f)aith

14. Circle each preposition in this sentence: The old rabbit (from) this fairytale lives (in) a dark pit (along with) twenty white elephants.
(16, 17)

15. Circle the abstract noun from this list: gardener, slugs, flowers, (peace), vegetables, rabbit
(7)

16. Circle the gerund from this sentence: My dog, Max, enjoys (digging.)
(19)

17. Circle the infinitive from this sentence: At night, he likes (to howl).
(23)

18. For a–c, circle the correct irregular verb form.
(14)
     (a) They (has, (have))   (b) I ((am) is, are)   (c) He (do, (does))

19. In the sentence below, circle the verb phrase and name its tense.
(21)

     Max (is fighting) the ferocious old rabbit.   ___present progressive___ tense

20. In the space to the right, diagram each word of this
(19, 27) sentence: My intelligent cousin enjoys reading.

Circle the correct word to complete sentences 1–6.

1. A prefix meaning "with" or "together" is (phobia-, (syn-), peri-).
(35)

2. A prefix meaning "around," "about," or "surrounding" is (miso-, eu-, (peri-)).
(25)

3. This sentence is (declarative, (imperative), interrogative, exclamatory): Run as fast as you can.
(1)

4. The word group below is a (sentence fragment, (run-on sentence), complete sentence).
(3)
        Uncle Remus told a story to a little seven-year-old boy he was the son of Miss Sally.

5. This word group is a (phrase, (clause)): because Brer Fox wanted to capture Brer Rabbit
(24)

6. The noun or pronoun that follows a preposition is called the (subject, (object), modifier) of the preposition.
(32)

7. Circle the concrete noun from this list: Italian, Japanese, Islam, philosophy, (rabbit), kindness, stealth
(7)

8. Circle the gerund from this sentence: (Swimming) is healthful exercise.
(19)

9. Write the plural of the noun *spy*. _____spies_____
(12, 13)

10. Circle each letter that should be capitalized in this sentence:
(20, 26) (l)ast (t)uesday, (m)other and (i) read, from the story "(u)ncle (r)emus," a rhyme that began, "(d)e place wharbouts you spill de grease…."

11. Circle the four prepositions from this sentence:
(16, 17) (Owing to) Brer Rabbit's skeptical nature, he successfully escaped (from) Brer Fox's cave (to) the closest bush (near) his rabbit hole.

12. Underline the prepositional phrase and circle the object of the preposition in this sentence: Brer Rabbit
(17, 32) pulled a calamus root <u>out of his</u> (dish)

13. Add periods where they are needed in this sentence: Mrs. Wang starts work at Pilgrim Ltd. every day at
(35) eight a.m. sharp.

14. Circle the word from this list that is *not* a helping verb: is, am, are, was, were, be, being, been, has, had,
(8) have, do, does, did, shall, will, (smell), should, would, can, could, may, might, must

15. Circle the linking verb in this sentence: The rabbit (appears) intelligent, for he cleverly outsmarts the fox.
(22)

16. For a–c, circle the correct irregular verb form.
(14) (a) we (was, (were))   (b) it (do, (does))   (c) you (has, (have))

For sentences 17 and 18, underline the verb and circle the direct object if there is one. Then underline "transitive" or "intransitive." (Hint: A "transitive" verb has a direct object.)

17. Brer Rabbit <u>will outsmart</u> (Brer Fox) time and time again. (<u>transitive</u>, intransitive)
(25, 31)

18. Brer Fox <u>will wait</u> along the path for Brer Rabbit. (transitive, <u>intransitive</u>)
(25, 31)

19. Circle the indirect object in this sentence: Brer Rabbit presents (Brer Fox) a delicious dinner.
(34)

20. Fill in the blank diagram to the right using
(32, 24) each word of this sentence: Uncle Remus told
        the child an amusing story about Brer Rabbit.

READ CAREFULLY   Name: _____

Circle the correct word to complete sentences 1–7.

1. The prefix (ante-, caco-, eu-) means before.
(31)

2. The prefix (peri-, tele-, an-) means far or distant.
(28)

3. This sentence is (declarative, imperative, interrogative, exclamatory): Have the sheep been sheared?
(1)

4. This word group is a (sentence fragment, run-on sentence, complete sentence): Clutch was greedy, his
(3) brother would have shared his last morsel with a hungry dog.

5. This word group is a (phrase, clause): until I see you
(24)

6. Coordinating (conjunctions, verbs, nouns) join parts of a sentence that are equal.
(36)

7. Correlative (nouns, adjectives, conjunctions) always come in pairs.
(38)

8. Write the plural of *piccolo*. ___piccolos___
(12, 13)

9. Write the correct verb form: The brother ___pities___ (present tense of *pity*) Clutch's sheep.
(6)

10. Circle each letter that should be capitalized in this sentence: (t)he teacher required each student to read (r)ay
(5, 20) (b)radbury's (t)he (m)artian (c)hronicles.

11. Underline each prepositional phrase from this sentence and circle the object of each preposition: Away
(17, 32) from their (fields), Clutch and his brother, Kind, discover a pasture of (violets) among the (grass).

12. Circle the word from this list that is *not* a helping verb: is, am, are, was, were, be, being, been, (here), has,
(8) have, had, may, might, must, can, could, do, does, did, shall, will, should, would

13. Circle each coordinating conjunction from this list: (and), (but), (yet), in, (or), on, (nor), (for), (so), do, did, rag
(36)

14. Circle the correlative conjunctions in this sentence: (Not only) the father (but also) the son lovingly sheared
(38) the sheep.

15. Circle the gerund in this sentence: The energetic flight attendant likes (traveling).
(19)

16. In this sentence, circle the verb phrase and name its tense: Kind (has sheared) the wolves!
(18) ___present perfect___ tense

17. Circle the linking verb in this sentence: Caleb hiked all day, but at dusk he (grew) weary.
(22)

18. Add periods where they are needed in this sentence:
(35)
          Mr. R. U. Greedy, Jr., has been counting money since three a.m.

Complete the diagrams of sentences 19 and 20.

19. The father gave the young shepherds good advice.
(28, 34)

20. The wool of sheep and wolves provides not only
(32, 38) warmth but also protection.

Circle the correct word(s) to complete sentences 1–5.

1. The prefix (*hypo-* *hyper-* *miso-*) means excessive.
(41)

2. The prefix (*hetero-* *homo-*) means different.
(44)

3. The following is a (sentence fragment, run-on sentence, complete sentence): Please listen to me.
(3)

4. This word group is a (phrase, clause): along with an eagle on top of a snow-covered mountain
(24)

5. Of the four Hake brothers, Bryon is the (older, oldest).
(42)

6. Circle the abstract noun from this list: Hinduism, United Kingdom, toenail, Professor Green
(7)

Circle each letter that should be capitalized in 7 and 8.

7. last june, i read an interesting short story called "a seller of dreams."
(11, 20)

8. dear miss stewart,
(26, 29)   did you know that there are many lutherans in the northeast?

                    warmly,
                    mallory

9. The plural of the noun *suffix* is ___suffixes___.
(12, 13)

10. Add commas and periods as needed to this sentence: Mrs. Crabtree promised to bring lettuce, tomatoes,
(35, 44) and cucumbers for our luncheon on Sunday, May 12.

11. Circle the verb phrase in this sentence and label its tense: Peter will be going to his aunt's house.
(21) _____future progressive_____ tense

12. For sentences a and b, circle the verb phrase and then circle action or linking.
(4, 22)
   (a) Does her voice sound sweet and melodious? (action, linking)

   (b) Has someone sounded a noisy alarm? (action, linking)

13. Circle the two possessive adjectives in this sentence: After the old seller's warning, Peter's intent was to
(28) rescue Aunt Jane.

14. Circle the correlative conjunctions in this sentence: Not only the guests but also Peter fled the castle.
(38)

15. Circle the predicate nominative in this sentence: The castle became a black shadow.
(39)

For 16–18, write whether the italicized noun is nominative, objective, or possessive case.

16. The man in golden shoes and a scarlet robe is the old *seller* of dreams. ___nominative___ case
(40)

17. The ancient castle lies under a terrible *enchantment*. ___objective___ case
(40)

18. Does *Peter's* frightening dream become a reality? ___possessive___ case
(40)

Complete the diagrams of sentences 19 and 20.

19. Her nephew, Peter, has a dream about an
(33, 45) enchanted castle.

20. His scary dream becomes significant and
(28, 41) meaningful.

Circle the correct word(s) to complete sentences 1–6.

1. The prefix ((pro-), re-, an-) means "before."
(30)

2. The prefix *hetero-* means (same, (different)).
(44)

3. The past participle of the verb *glare* is ((glared), glaring).
(15)

4. The following is a (complete sentence, (run-on sentence), sentence fragment):
(3)

        I read a poem it was written by Robert Frost.

5. Of the two stories, William Faulkner's is the ((more), most) interesting.
(43)

6. ((Do), Does) our country have many allies in the fight against terrorism?
(14)

7. Circle each coordinating conjunction in this sentence: We walked, (but) she drove, (so) she arrived sooner.
(36)

8. Circle each gerund in this sentence: Theater students usually practice (singing), (dancing), and (acting).
(18)

9. Write the plural of the noun *peach*. _____peaches_____
(12, 13)

10. Circle the appositive in this sentence: In an old, Anglo-Saxon epic poem, a Scandinavian prince, (Beowulf),
(45) rids the Danes of a dreaded monster.

11. Circle each letter that should be capitalized in this sentence: (w)ith his family, (r)obert (f)rost sailed across the
(5, 29) (a)tlantic (o)cean to (e)ngland.

12. Circle the infinitive in this sentence: Unfortunately, the sea lions refused (to perform) in front of the crowd.
(23, 48)

13. Underline each prepositional phrase circling the object of each preposition in this sentence: <u>From among</u>
(17, 32) <u>many talented American (poets)</u> Robert Frost is the most admired poet <u>of the twentieth (century)</u>.

14. In the following sentence, circle the verb phrase and name its tense: Fortunately, the antidote (has)
(18) (counteracted) the effects of the poison. _____present perfect_____ tense

15. For sentences a and b, circle the verb phrase and then circle transitive or intransitive.
(21, 31)
   (a) The prolific poet (has been writing) several hundred poems each year. ((transitive), intransitive)

   (b) The prolific poet (has been writing) throughout the entire night. (transitive, (intransitive))

16. Circle the sentence below that is written correctly.
(47)
      He likes that kind of a novel.   (He likes that kind of novel.)

17. Add periods and commas as needed in this sentence: Mrs. May B. Smart teaches violin lessons on
(35) Mondays, Wednesdays, Fridays, and Saturdays.

18. Tell whether the italicized word in this sentence is nominative, objective, or possessive case: The 1930s
(40) brought one *tragedy* after another for Robert Frost. _____objective_____ case

19. Underline the pronouns and circle their antecedent in this sentence: (Robert Frost) lost <u>his</u> youngest
(49) daughter in 1934, <u>his</u> wife in 1938, and <u>his</u> son in 1940.

20. Complete the diagram of this sentence:
(39, 48) Robert Frost is the poet to read.

Circle the best word(s) to complete sentences 1–5.

1. The expression, "the tongue is a fire," is a (pathos, caricature, (figure of speech)).
(54)

2. The Greek root *anthropos* means (loving, angled, (human)).
(53)

3. Of the two poems, this one by Langston Hughes is the (good, (better), best).
(43)

4. The man on the phone was ((he), him).
(53, 54)

5. Racial prejudice mattered to (he, (him))
(53, 54)

6. Underline each prepositional phrase and circle the object of each preposition in this sentence:
(16, 32)
    In (one) of his (poems), he reflects on (blacks) being sold down the (river) into (slavery)

7. Circle the verb phrase in this sentence, and then circle transitive or intransitive:
(31)
    (Did) Langston Hughes (respond) with surprise at his class's choice of him as the class poet? (transitive, (intransitive))

8. Write the (a) past tense and (b) past participle of the irregular verb *shrink*.
(15, 52)

    (a) ____shrank____   (b) ____(has) shrunk____

9. Add commas and periods as needed in this sentence:
(35, 46)
    Ernest's father, Dr. Clarence Hemingway, gave Ernest a fishing pole, a net, and new boots.

10. Circle the coordinating conjunction in this sentence: Langston Hughes was a playwright, a novelist, a
(36) song lyricist, (and) a poet.

11. In this sentence, circle the pronoun and name its case: Unfortunately, (she) seems as personable as a marble
(53) statue. ____nominative____ case

12. Write the plural of the noun *eulogy*. ____eulogies____
(12, 13)

13. Circle each third person plural pronoun from this list: he, him, she, her, (they), (them), we, us, you
(51)

14. Circle each objective case pronoun from this list: (me), (him), I, she, (them), they, he, (her), we, (us)
(54)

15. Circle each letter that should be capitalized in this sentence: (y)es, (i) believe that (l)angston (h)ughes wrote a
(5, 20) poem titled "(t)he (n)egro (s)peaks of (r)ivers."

16. Circle the verb phrase in this sentence and name its tense: (Was) that elephant (winking) at you and me?
(21) ____past progressive____ tense

17. Circle the infinitive in this sentence: I think it is time (to discuss) figures of speech.
(23, 48)

18. Circle each possessive noun from this list: (person's), persons, bosses, (boss's), (bosses')
(9, 56)

19. Write the second person singular or plural personal pronoun. ____you____
(51)

20. Diagram this sentence: Editing and translating interested this man of many passions.
(19, 33)

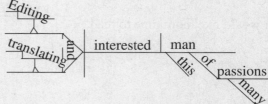

Circle the correct words to complete sentences 1–9.

1. The prefix *poly-* means (shape, angle, (many)).
(57)

2. The Greek word *pseudo* means (real, (pretend), love).
(60)

3. The following word group is a ((phrase) clause): Eugene O'Neill, America's first great playwright
(24)

4. Of Eugene O'Neill's many plays, I think *The Iceman Cometh.* is the (more, (most)) captivating.
(43)

5. A predicate ((adjective), nominative, preposition) follows a linking verb and describes the subject.
(41)

6. Unfortunately, the wandering beagle has lost (it's, (its)) collar.
(56)

7. His brother and (him, (he)) worked on plays together.
(53, 54)

8. The italicized words in this sentence are ((participles) gerunds): The *barking* beagle disturbed my *sleeping* sister.
(58)

9. Have you (spoke, (spoken)) to your best friend today?
(52)

10. Write the plural of *ally.* _____allies_____
(12, 13)

11. Circle the entire verb phrase in this sentence and name its tense: Riveted to the story, Jed (had been reading) for three hours. ___past perfect progressive___ tense
(21)

12. Add periods and commas as needed in this sentence and circle each letter that should be capitalized: (n)o, (mr.) (w)ang, (i) have never run a marathon. (t)wenty-six miles is too far.
(5, 35)

13. Circle the appositive in this sentence: Benjamin Franklin, (a brilliant statesman,) helped to create the Constitution of the United States of America.
(45)

14. Circle the infinitive in this sentence: After three hours of reading the textbook, Jed began (to snore)
(23)

15. Underline the dependent clause and circle the subordinating conjunction in this sentence: (Even though) Eugene O'Neill was a successful playwright, his personal life was unhappy.
(57)

16. Circle each objective case personal pronoun from this list:
(54)
(me)   (him)   I   she   (them)   they   he   (her)   we   (us)

17. Circle the gerund phrase in this sentence: Following the recipe, Stacy tried (cooking a new Chinese dish)
(58)

18. Underline each prepositional phrase and circle the object of each preposition in this sentence: On account of the (drought) water use in our (county) is restricted during the hot (part) of the (day)
(16, 32)

Diagram sentences 19 and 20 in the space to the right.

19. Bursting with creative energy, Eugene O'Neill wrote many plays.
(25, 59)

20. I would like more time to read.
(28, 48)

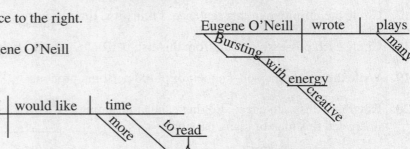

Circle the correct words to complete sentences 1–10.

1. In the last battle, the victory will be (our's, (ours)).
(56)

2. Sue's sister and (her, (she)) will travel together.
(53, 54)

3. (Connotation, (Denotation)) is the literal, or dictionary, meaning.
(61)

4. The Greek root (mania, morphe, (biblion)) means book.
(64)

5. The following word group is a (phrase, (clause)): as she carried the heavy pitchers to the soldiers
(24)

6. Of the two newspaper articles, this one is the ((more), most) accurate.
(43)

7. A ((subordinating), coordinating) conjunction introduces a dependent clause.
(57)

8. The italicized words in this sentence are (participles, (gerunds)): Benito likes *singing* and *dancing*.
(58)

9. Have you (chose, (chosen)) your friends wisely?
(52)

10. Augustina, Mary Ambree, and Molly Pitcher took it upon (theirselves, (themselves)) to fight for their
(60) countries.

11. Write the plural of *fistful*. _____fistfuls_____
(9)

12. In the blank, write the correct verb form: Penelope _____has worn_____ her sister's clothes all
(18) week.   present perfect tense of *wear*

13. Add periods and commas as needed in this sentence and circle each letter that should be capitalized: (y)es,
(11, 20) (i) heard (d)r. (c)hew say, "(y)ou need to drink more water, lose some weight, and eat a variety of fruits and vegetables."

14. Underline the dependent clause and circle the subordinating conjunction in this sentence: Molly Pitcher
(57) fired her husband's cannon (until) the British were defeated.

15. Circle each adjective in this sentence: (The) day after (the) (furious) battle of Monmouth, (a) (sad-faced) widow
(27, 28) had (swollen) eyes.

16. Circle the appositive in this sentence: Molly Pitcher, (a brave volunteer) received a sergeant's commission
(45) and half-pay for life.

17. Circle each nominative case personal pronoun from this list:
(53)
     me   him   (I)   (she)   them   (they)   (he)   her   (we)   us

18. Underline the participial phrase in this sentence and circle the word it modifies: That noisy, two-engine
(59) (airplane) circling the mountain peak disturbed the peaceful slumber of the campers in the forest.

Diagram sentences 19 and 20 in the space to the right.

19. The neighbor who gave me the squash likes
(59, 64) growing vegetables.

20. She prepares the soil, and her husband plants the
(4, 62) seeds.

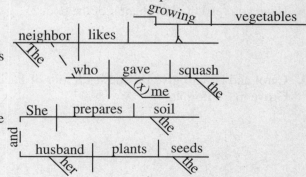

Circle the correct word to complete sentences 1–10.

1. (Who's, (Whose)) novel is this?
(64)

2. Joe's dad and (him, (he)) went hiking.
(53, 54)

3. (Who, (Whom)) are you calling?
(64)

4. Kate swims faster than (me, (I)).
(53, 54)

5. The Greek root (*biblion, mania, (metron)*) means measure.
(67)

6. The Greek root *chroma* means (large, sound, (color)).
(69)

7. The following word group is a ((phrase), clause): a description of the miserable conditions in migrant labor
(24) camps

8. Of the two automobiles, this one is the ((more), most) reliable.
(43)

9. The neighbors' house, ((which), that) sold yesterday, has two small bedrooms and a large swimming pool.
(64)

10. John Steinbeck and his wife typed and edited the novels (theirselves, (themselves)).
(60)

11. Write the plural of *dish*. _____ dishes _____
(12, 13)

12. In the blank, write the correct verb form: Carolyn _____ is spinning _____ wool from her sheep in
(21) order to make yarn for a blanket.   present progressive tense of *spin*

13. Add periods and commas as needed in this sentence and circle each letter that should be capitalized:
(20, 35) (Y)esterday, (J)ohn explained, "(K)eyboards, mice, printers, and monitors are all peripherals of computers."

14. Underline the dependent clause and circle the subordinating conjunction in this sentence: *The Grapes of*
(57) *Wrath* is required reading in many schools (since) it is regarded as an American classic.

15. Add quotation marks as needed in this sentence: "Software," said John, "is made up of instructions that
(68, 69) tell a computer what to do."

16. Circle the appositive in this sentence: *The Grapes of Wrath,* (an influential book,) leaves its mark on
(45) generation after generation.

17. Circle the gerund phrase in this sentence: Unfortunately, (missing the train) caused me to miss my flight
(58) home from Germany.

18. Underline the participial phrase in this sentence and circle the word it modifies: The weary (traveler)
(59) standing in the rain has been waiting seven hours for a bus to the train station.

Diagram sentences 19 and 20 in the space to the right.

19. Have you read the last chapter of the book?
(28, 33)

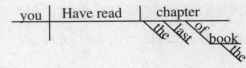

20. Carol and he will give Ed and her a tour of Pacific
(34, 37) Grove in California.

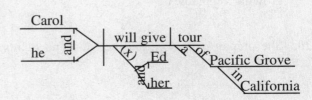

Circle the correct word(s) to complete sentences 1–10.

1. The Greek word *derma* means (god, same, (skin)).   **2.** A (stereotype, (pun), satire) is a play on words.
(71)   *(72)*

3. (Who, (Whom)) were you expecting?   **4.** I ate more zuccchini than (him, (he)).
(64)   *(53, 66)*

5. Mom and ((I), me) shall visit our elderly friends at the convalescent hospital.
(53, 54)

6. Because of the storm, ((we), us) passengers felt turbulence throughout the flight.
(53, 56)

7. The underlined clause in the following sentence is ((essential), nonessential): The book <u>that some readers</u>
(65) <u>like best</u> is Edith Wharton's *Age of Innocence*.

8. The book, ((which), that) can be found in the fiction section, costs $15.95.
(65)

9. Last summer, I (builded, (built)) a magnificent sand castle at the beach.
(75)

10. Each of the ladies (want, (wants)) (their, (her)) own dog to win the herding contest.
(56, 71)

11. Write the plural of *entry*. ____entries_____
(12, 13)

12. In the blank, write the correct verb form: Carolyn ____had brought_____ her pet emu to the
(18) country fair.   past perfect tense of *bring*

13. Add periods and commas as needed in this sentence and circle each letter that should be capitalized: (W)e
(5, 35) think that (m)r. (C)rockett, a fellow traveler, may have accidentally picked up (t)om's suitcase at the train
station in (l)ondon, (e)ngland.

14. Underline the dependent clause and circle the subordinating conjunction in this sentence: I read Edith
(57) Wharton's *Ethan Frome* (because) <u>my teacher recommended it</u>.

15. Add quotation marks as needed in this sentence: "Character is doing the right thing when no one is
(68, 69) looking," said Congressman J.C. Watts.

16. Underline each word that should be italicized in this sentence: I read her first poems in a magazine called
(72) <u>The Atlantic Monthly</u>.

17. Circle the gerund phrase in this sentence: (Following my neighbor's excellent directions) enabled me to
(58) find my way to your house.

18. Underline the participial phrase in this sentence and circle the word it modifies: <u>Having bitten into a sour</u>
(59) <u>peach</u>, (Homer) grimaced.

Diagram sentences 19 and 20 in the space to the right.

19. Neither of the gentlemen knows his itinerary.
(33, 71)

20. Agnes and she brought me some fresh lemons.
(34, 37)

Circle the correct word(s) to complete sentences 1–10.

1. The Greek root *therap* means (heat, fire, (cure)).
(79)

2. Hope is the ((antithesis), synonym) of despair.
(78)

3. Neither of the students (know, (knows)) the rules.
(77, 78)

4. I grew more tomatoes than ((they), them).
(53, 66)

5. (Me and Dad, Dad and me, (Dad and I)) will meet you and (she, (her)) at the natural history museum.
(53, 54)

6. Fern, would you please invite (we, (us)) goslings to Wilbur's birthday party?
(56, 60)

7. The underlined clause in the following sentence is (essential, (nonessential)): *Charlotte's Web*, <u>which is a</u>
(65) <u>children's story</u>, tells about a kindly spider and a doomed pig, Wilbur the runt.

8. Wilbur has (lied, lay, (lain)) on that straw all morning.
(75)

9. One of the pilots (fly, (flies)) ((their, his/her)) own plane around the world each spring.
(80)

10. The spider ((that), which) counsels Wilbur is named Charlotte.
(65)

11. Write the plural of *self*. _____selves_____
(60)

12. In the blank, write the correct verb form: E. B. White _____has written_____ some magnificent
(18) stories about farm life and its animals.   present perfect tense of *write*

13. Add punctuation marks as needed in the following and circle each letter that should be capitalized:
(20, 44) (C)harlotte's (W)eb is about friendship, affection, protection, and adventure. (H)ave you read it?

14. Underline the dependent clause and circle the subordinating conjunction in this sentence: The author
(57) provides local color (as) <u>he describes animals, insects, sights, and sounds on the farm</u>.

15. Add quotation marks as needed in this sentence: Mrs. Poovey has written a delightful essay titled
(68, 69) "Crawling Critters on the Bank of Coot's Creek."

16. Underline each word that should be italicized in this sentence: The French say that E. B. White's essays
(72) are <u>très bien</u>.

17. Circle the two gerund phrases in this sentence: (Spinning fancy, miraculous webs) is Charlotte's way of
(58) (communicating with her friends).

18. Underline the participial phrase in this sentence and circle the word it modifies: <u>Cradling the pig in her</u>
(59) <u>arms</u>, (Fern) feeds Wilbur with a baby bottle.

Diagram sentences 19 and 20 in the space to the right.

19. The heroine of the story is Charlotte, a spider in the
(33, 45) barn.

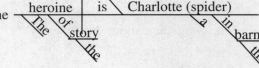

20. The stories of E. B. White feature talking animals
(33, 48) with human feelings.

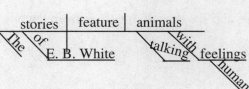

Circle the correct word(s) to complete sentences 1–10.

1. The Greek root (*therap-*, *cosmos*, (*thermos*)) means "heat." **2.** *Psyche* refers to one's (eyes, body, (mind)).
(85)   (83)

3. He (don't, (doesn't)) have (no, (any)) regrets.   **4.** We have more earthworms than ((they) them).
(14, 81)   (66)

5. (Me and Mom, Mom and me, (Mom and I)) might see you and ((him) he) at the theater.
(53, 54)

6. (Us, (We)) drama students are studying our parts for the play.
(65)

7. The underlined clause in the following sentence is (essential, (nonessential)): *Pilgrim*, <u>which is coming</u>
(65) <u>soon to the theater</u>, will capture the attention of people of all ages.

8. Tennessee Williams ((drew) drawn) recognition as a playwright during the 1940s and 1950s.
(73)

9. (Do, (Does)) one of your relatives have (their, (his/her)) office in Tennessee?
(77, 80)

10. I haven't ((ever) never) (saw, (seen)) Tennessee Williams's *The Glass Menagerie* performed on stage.
(81)

11. Write the plural of *allegory*. _____allegories_____
(12, 13)

12. In the blank, write the correct verb form: The author _____has woven_____ much realism into
(18) the story.   present perfect tense of *weave*

For 13 and 14, add quotation marks and punctuation marks as needed. Also, circle each letter that should be capitalized.

13. "(i) knew from his accent that (t)ennessee (w)illiams came from the (s)outh," said (m)rs. (p)oovey.
(29, 68)

14. "(b)efore (i) go to the theater," said (m)r. (p)oovey, "(i) must purchase the tickets, wash the car, and mend my torn
(68, 69) tuxedo."

15. Underline the dependent clause and circle the subordinating conjunction in this sentence: <u>(Since) it takes</u>
(57) <u>place in an existing district of New Orleans</u>, *A Street Car Named Desire* contains realism.

16. Underline each word that should be italicized in this sentence: Tennessee Williams sold his first story,
(72) "The Vengeance of Nitocris," to <u>Weird Tales</u>, a widely circulated magazine.

17. Circle the gerund phrase in this sentence: Having received a typewriter for his eleventh birthday, Stuart
(58) stopped (writing longhand).

18. Underline the participial phrase in this sentence and circle the word it modifies: <u>Having received a</u>
(59) <u>computer for his twenty-first birthday</u>, (Stuart) stopped using the typewriter.

Diagram sentences 19 and 20 in the space to the right.

19. Writing an effective drama may take many years.
(25, 59)

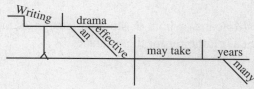

20. Stuart quickly typed his story about pandemonium
(35, 83) behind the stage.

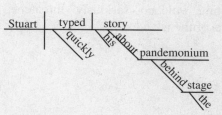

Circle the correct word(s) to complete sentences 1–10.

1. The Greek root *osteo* means (form, world, (bone)).
(89)

2. Psychology studies the (earth, (mind), universe).
(83)

3. She (don't, (doesn't)) want (no, (any)) help.
(81)

4. She ((isn't), ain't, aren't) as tall as (me, (I)).
(66, 80)

5. (Me and you, You and me, (You and I)) shall meet Rob and (he, (him)) at the library.
(53, 54)

6. The word *not* is an (adjective, (adverb), appositive).
(89)

7. The underlined part of this sentence is a(n) ((essential), nonessential) part: In the fresco, the man <u>who is</u>
(65) <u>holding a mackerel</u> is a Cretan fisherman.

8. Hector plays basketball (good, (well)). He plays a ((good), well) game of basketball.
(84)

9. The Minoan civilization, on the island of Crete, had (it's, (its)) own script, called *Linear A*.
(56)

10. I haven't ((ever), never) (saw, (seen)) the island of Crete.
(81)

11. Write the comparative form of the adverb *peacefully*. _____ more peacefully _____
(90)

12. In the blank, write the correct verb form: Archaeologists _____ are searching _____ for large jars that
(21) once held grain or olive oil in the palace.   present progressive tense of *search*

For 13 and 14, add quotation marks and punctuation marks as needed, circle each letter that should be capitalized, and underline each part that should be italicized.

13. (p)rofessor (m)inos asked me, "(d)o you remember from your reading in (b)arker's (w)orld (h)istory what major
(68, 72) crops the (m)inoans raised?"

14. "(Y)es, (p)rofessor (m)inos," (i)answered, "the major crops were wheat, barley, vegetables, grapes, and olives."
(11, 68)

15. Underline the dependent clause and circle the subordinating conjunction in this sentence: We shall sail to
(57) the island of Crete <u>(as soon as) everyone has boarded the ship.</u>

16. Add hyphens where they are needed in this sentence: Twenty-two plus twenty-one equals forty-three.
(85, 87)

17. Circle the gerund phrase in this sentence: The archeologist purchased a new shovel for (digging the ancient
(58) ruins.)

18. Underline the participial phrase in this sentence and circle the word it modifies: <u>Digging around ancient</u>
(59) <u>Minoan palaces,</u> (archaeologists) have uncovered old thrones and decorations.

Diagram sentences 19 and 20 in the space to the right.

19. The Minoans, whom I studied, designed highly
(64, 89) efficient plumbing for their palaces.

20. An erupting volcano seriously threatened the
(33, 48) inhabitants of the island.

Circle the correct word(s) to complete sentences 1–10.

1. The word *sure* is an (adjective, adverb).
(89, 92)

2. The word *really* is an (adjective, adverb).
(89, 92)

3. A hexapod has (four, five, six) legs.
(92)

4. Is Ishani feeling (well, good) today?
(84)

5. The Greek prefix *deka-* means (bad, not, ten).
(94)

6. Can't (nobody, anybody) decipher the script used by the Harappa people in India?
(81)

7. (Beside, Besides) growing vegetables and grains, the Harappas might have been the first people to grow cotton.
(95)

8. The italicized word in this sentence is an (adjective, adverb): We're studying *early* civilizations.
(27, 88)

9. The italicized word in this sentence is an (adjective, adverb): We arrived *early* to hear the lecture.
(27, 88)

10. Maribel hasn't (ever, never) (saw, seen) the Indus Valley where the Harappas lived long ago.
(81)

11. Write the superlative form of the adverb *artfully*. _____most artfully_____
(90)

12. Circle the conjunctive adverb in this sentence: The Harappas had no modern plumbing; however, they created brick lavatories connected by chutes to a main drain.
(91)

For 13 and 14, circle each letter that should be capitalized, and add punctuation marks as needed.

13. Professor Trinh wrote an article called "Solving the Harappa Mystery," for he had dug among the ruins along with a team of archeologists from Boston, Massachusetts.
(50, 69)

14. "We have found Harappa pottery in Mesopotamia," said Professor Trinh, "so we know that these people traded their goods."
(30, 68)

15. Insert a colon where it is needed in this sentence: The Harappa farmers grew the following crops: cotton, wheat, barley, and vegetables.
(93)

16. Underline each word that should be italicized in this sentence: Professor Trinh has published several interesting articles in our local newspaper, the Mud Valley Gazette.
(72)

17. Circle the gerund phrase in this sentence: The Harappas enjoyed living in pleasant mud-brick houses.
(58)

18. Underline the participial phrase in this sentence and circle the word it modifies: Defending themselves with large clay missiles, the Harappas survived until about 1700 B.C.
(59)

Diagram sentences 19 and 20 in the space to the right.

19. Yesterday, the archeologists dug deep into the ruins for ancient relics.
(88, 94)

20. Future excavating will give us additional information about the Harappas' daily lives.
(34, 59)

Circle the correct word(s) to complete sentences 1–10.

1. The word (real, (really)) is an adverb.
(92)

2. Down the street ((come), comes) two ponies.
(6)

3. The Latin prefix *soli-* means (first, bone, (alone)).
(99)

4. A multitude is a great (king, (many), idea).
(96)

5. The italicized part of this sentence is a(n) (essential, (nonessential)) part: Anatolia, *which is now called*
(65) *Turkey*, was divided into several kingdoms, each with its own ruler.

6. The italicized part of this sentence is a(n) (noun, adjective, (adverb)) phrase: *During the period from 2500*
(99) *to 2000 BC,* the Egyptians built more large structures than other people in the Middle East.

7. Only two people in the class, you and (me, (I)), will make an Egyptian water clock for our display.
(53, 54)

8. A dependent clause may be connected to an independent clause by a (coordinating, (subordinating))
(57) conjunction.

9. The following sentence is (simple, compound, (complex), compound-complex): Although the people of
(100) Anatolia were among the world's first farmers, they amassed most of their wealth through trading metal.

10. I can't find that information (nowhere, (anywhere)) in my history book.
(81)

11. Write the comparative form of the adverb *imaginatively.* ___more imaginatively___
(90)

12. Circle the conjunctive adverb in this sentence: King Tut had fabulous riches; (however), no amount of
(91) wealth could extend his life.

For 13 and 14, circle each letter that should be capitalized, and add punctuation marks as needed.

13. (b)en said, "(h)ey, (g)randpa, the exhibit of (k)ing (t)ut's tomb is coming to (p)lano, (t)exas, on (s)unday, (n)ovember 17,
(44, 46) 2003."

14. (m)oses begged the pharaoh, "(l)et my people go."
(20, 46)

15. Write the possessive form of *Moses.* ___Moses's___
(97)

16. Underline each word that should be italicized in this sentence: In our entymology textbook, we can read all
(72) about locusts by looking up their scientific name, <u>locusta.</u>

17. Circle the infinitive phrase in this sentence: After the invasion of the Hyksos, the Egyptians learned (to use
(96) horses and chariots.)

18. In this sentence, underline the participial phrase and circle the word it modifies: (Scholars) <u>studying</u>
(59) <u>papyrus rolls</u> can learn a great deal about Egyptian life.

Diagram sentences 19 and 20 in the space to the right.

19. In 1503 BC, Queen Hatshepsut became one of the
(39, 94) few women pharoahs.

20. Cooking outside prevented hazardous fires in
(28, 59) Egyptian homes.

Circle the correct word(s) to complete sentences 1–9.

1. José didn't ((believe), beleive) my tall tale.
(110)

2. Marta and ((he), him) laughed at my fabrication.
(53, 54)

3. The prefix ((trans-), inter-, extra-) means across.
(109)

4. The prefix *inter-* means (against, (between), not).
(108)

5. The italicized part of this sentence is a(n) (essential, (nonessential)) part: The driver, *Nick*, skillfully
(65)   maneuvered the ambulance through the traffic.

6. The italicized part of this sentence is a(n) (noun, (adjective), adverb) clause: My grandmother won't do
(99)   anything *that might increase her chances of having a stroke*.

7. There were no arguments (between, (among)) the six teammates.
(95)

8. I haven't ((ever), never) seen a roadrunner in this part of the country. Have you?
(81)

9. The following sentence is ((simple), compound, complex, compound-complex): Because of a bystander's
(100) screaming for help, the victim had more than one rescuer.

10. Underline the dependent clause and circle the subordinating conjunction in this sentence: Good Samaritan
(57)   Laws allow us to protect ourselves legally (when) we assist ill or injured persons.

11. Write the superlative form of the adverb *imaginatively*. ___most imaginatively___
(90)

12. Circle the conjunctive adverb in this sentence: Seek shelter if a thunderstorm approaches; (however), if no
(91)   shelter is available, get into a car and roll up the windows.

For 13 and 14, circle each letter that should be capitalized, and add punctuation marks as needed.

13. (U)ncontrollable risk factors for stroke are age, gender, and family history. (R)egular exercise reduces one's
(44, 63) chance of stroke, for it increases blood circulation.

14. (W)hen you call for help, you should give the dispatcher the victim's location, condition, and name.
(50, 63)

15. Write the possessive form of *roses*. ___roses'___
(97)

16. Combine this word and suffix to make a new word: *drop* + *ed* ___dropped___
(108, 109)

17. On the line below, rewrite this sentence using active voice: Angela is surprised by the gift.
(102)
_____The gift surprised Angela._____

18. Which sentence is clearer? Circle A or B. B
(50, 103)
      A. The trailblazer found a downed power line hiking down the path.
      B. Hiking down the path, the trailblazer found a downed power line.

Diagram sentences 19 and 20 in the space to the right.

19. Learning CPR might enable you to save a life.
(59, 96)

20. Now is the time to prepare for a future emergency.
(39, 96)

More Practice Lesson 2

Circle the simple subject and underline the simple predicate in each sentence. If the subject is understood, write "(you)" after the sentence.

1. Are (vegetables) nutritious?

2. Please pass the broccoli.   (you)

3. (Spinach) contains iron.

4. My (rabbit) hates carrots.

5. (He) prefers alfalfa.

6. (Blanca) fried some yucca.

7. Will (you) stay for dinner?

8. Have (you) eaten your vegetables?

9. (James) has eaten four servings.

10. Please taste the delicious zucchini. (you)

11. Where are the (green beans)?

12. (Robert) has hidden them under a napkin.

13. Do (you) like sweet potatoes?

14. (Isabel) baked some in the oven last night.

15. Frozen (peas) in a bag make a good ice pack for injuries.

16. The (chef) with the tall white hat went home.

17. Will (he) return tomorrow?

18. Would (you) like more squash or mashed potatoes?

19. This summer, (I) have been growing cucumbers.

20. Here comes (dessert)!

Circle each letter that should be capitalized in these sentences.

1. asia, the largest continent in the world, is connected by land to europe.

2. therefore, europe and asia together are often called eurasia.

3. the second largest continent is africa.

4. north america and south america are next in size after africa.

5. they are separated from europe, asia, and africa by the atlantic ocean and the pacific ocean.

6. north and south america were once connected by the isthmus of panama, but the panama canal now separates these continents.

7. the frozen continent of antarctica lies at the bottom of the world.

8. the continent of europe is in the eastern hemisphere.

9. china, india, and pakistan are also in the eastern hemisphere.

10. john and james attended pasadena city college in california.

11. mr. rivas studies greek and hebrew at princeton theological seminary.

12. mr. torres has lived in memphis, tennessee; alberta, canada; and quito, ecuador.

13. the amazon river runs through brazil in south america.

14. this june we will hike in the rocky mountains.

15. el salvador, guatemala, honduras, and costa rica are part of central america.

16. did mr. tseng visit havana, cuba last tuesday?

17. have you seen the empire state building in new york city?

18. the london bridge now stands at lake havasu.

19. the months of july and august are hot and dry in the mojave desert.

More Practice Lesson 8

Underline the entire verb phrase in each sentence.

1. Laura Ingalls <u>was born</u> in 1867 in the country outside Minneapolis.

2. Her parents <u>had grown</u> up on the Wisconsin frontier.

3. Her mother, Caroline, <u>may have been</u> the first white newborn in Brookfield outside Milwaukee.

4. Laura's parents <u>had joined</u> the westward pioneer movement into the vast Dakota prairie.

5. At that time, the U. S. government <u>was giving</u> Dakota farmland to pioneer families.

6. Laura's family <u>must have been</u> the first residents of De Smet, South Dakota.

7. Laura <u>had started</u> her book in the 1920s.

8. *Little House in the Big Woods* <u>was published</u> in 1931.

9. <u>Have</u> you <u>read</u> this novel?

10. It <u>may have been</u> the most popular children's story at that time.

11. Young readers <u>must have been</u> curious.

12. What <u>would happen</u> next?

13. The country <u>has changed</u> since Laura's time.

14. The Big Woods <u>have vanished</u>.

15. The Ingalls clan <u>had remained</u> a poor, homesteading family.

16. Charles Ingalls <u>was known</u> for his scrupulous fairness.

17. He <u>had been hired</u> by the Chicago and Northwestern railroad.

18. <u>Have</u> you <u>visited</u> the Laura Ingalls Wilder Museum?

More Practice Lesson 20

Circle each letter that should be capitalized in these sentences.

1. (w)e remember (s)ir (t)homas (M)ore for his literary work (u)topia, which describes an imaginary ideal society.

2. (a)braham (l)incoln said, "(t)ruth is generally the best vindication against slander."

3. (h)ave you read the poem "(p)aul (r)evere's (r)ide" by (h)enry (w)adsworth (l)ongfellow?

4. (r)alph (w)aldo (e)merson wrote, "(i)t is better to suffer injustice than to do it."

5. (g)eoffrey (c)haucer's (t)he (c)anterbury (t)ales shows the life of fourteenth-century (e)nglish society.

6. (h)enry (w)ard (b)eecher once said, "(i)t is not work that kills men; it is worry."

7. (i)n (t)he (b)ook (o)f (m)artyrs, (j)ohn (f)oxe wrote about martyrs of the (c)hristian church.

8. (r)obert (l)eighton said, "(g)od's choice acquaintances are humble [people]."

9. (i)n the late 1500s, (e)dmund (s)penser wrote his masterpiece, (t)he (f)aerie (q)ueen, an allegorical, epic romance.

10. (c)urious, (b)enito asked, "(w)hy did (d)elilah cut (s)amson's hair?

11. (p)resident (d)wight (d). (e)isenhower said, "(t)he spirit of man is more important than mere physical strength, and the spiritual fiber of a nation than its wealth."

12. (a) (p)uritan named (j)ohn (t)rapp once said, "(c)onscience is (g)od's spy and man's overseer."

13. (l)ike (s)penser's (f)aerie (q)ueen, (j)ohn (b)unyan's (p)ilgrim's (p)rogress is an allegory, a narrative in which the characters and places are symbols.

14. (i). (e)lectric energy   (ii). radiant energy
    a. (c)harge   a. (l)ight
    b. (c)ircuits   b. (c)olors

15. (i)n the book of (h)ebrews, (g)od promises, "(i) will never leave you, nor forsake you."

Circle each letter that should be capitalized in these sentences.

1. (i) think (a)unt (s)ukey puts green beans in her apple pies.

2. (h)ave you ever taken (p)rofessor (c)uilty's world history class?

3. (m)iss (f)arris teaches (e)nglish at (a)rroyo (h)igh (s)chool.

4. (d)o (g)randma and (g)randpa (p)etersen speak (d)anish?

5. (o)n (s)unday, (f)ather (o)'rourke recited the (c)atholic mass in (l)atin.

6. (w)ill (m)om meet (a)unt (c)hristie for breakfast?

7. (a)t the hospital, (r)abbi (c)ohen comforted the grieving family by reading from the (t)orah.

8. (t)he (k)oran is (i)slam's holy book.

9. (i) believe (d)r. (b)ebb is a surgeon at (h)untington (m)emorial (h)ospital.

10. (h)as (l)ieutenant (m)ussuli retired from the (u).(s). (a)ir (f)orce?

11. (a)fter a 12-month tour of duty, (c)aptain (r)ice returned from the (p)ersian (g)ulf.

12. (h)e had written many letters to his mother in (w)yoming.

13. (t)he (a)rabic term for (g)od is (a)llah.

14. (m)ost (m)uslims believe in repaying evil with good.

15. (b)oth (c)hristians and (m)uslims believe in a final judgment of (g)od.

16. (i)n (a)pril, (u)ncle (w)illiam will fly from (a)lbany, (n)ew (y)ork to (a)nchorage, (a)laska.

17. (j)enan and (j)umana baked (a)rmenian bread for their sister (n)adia.

18. (y)esterday, (d)r. (i)riye talked to (q)uan about (j)apanese history.

19. (i) heard that (c)ousin (n)ancy has a (r)ussian wolfhound.

20. (w)as (p)resident (i)shigaki in favor of the new statute in our club's by-laws?

Underline each adjective in these sentences.

1. <u>Three</u> <u>main</u> <u>climate</u> zones include <u>the</u> <u>frigid</u> zone, <u>the</u> <u>temperate</u> zone, and <u>the</u> <u>torrid</u> zone.

2. <u>The</u> <u>polar</u> climate of <u>the</u> <u>frigid</u> zone causes <u>a</u> <u>frozen</u> <u>ice</u> cap throughout <u>the</u> <u>entire</u> year.

3. In <u>the</u> <u>tundra</u> climate of <u>this</u> <u>frigid</u> zone, <u>some</u> plants will grow, but <u>no</u> trees will grow.

4. <u>The</u> <u>taiga</u> climate of <u>the</u> <u>temperate</u> zone allows for <u>vast</u> forests of <u>conifer</u> trees.

5. <u>The</u> <u>marine</u> climate has <u>moderate</u> temperatures and <u>much</u> rain and is found on <u>west</u> coasts of <u>some</u> continents.

6. <u>The</u> <u>continental</u> steppe is <u>a</u> <u>treeless</u> plain with <u>cold</u> winters, <u>hot</u> summers, and <u>little</u> rainfall.

7. In <u>the</u> interiors of <u>some</u> continents, we find <u>the</u> <u>humid</u> <u>continental</u> climate with <u>hot</u> summers, <u>cold</u> winters, and <u>much</u> rainfall.

8. <u>The</u> <u>humid</u> <u>subtropic</u> climate has <u>hot</u>, <u>moist</u> summers, <u>mild</u> winters, <u>thick</u> forests, and <u>dense</u> populations.

9. <u>This</u> climate is found on <u>east</u> coasts of continents.

10. <u>The</u> <u>subtropical</u> desert, on <u>the</u> <u>other</u> hand, produces <u>hot</u>, <u>dry</u> summers and <u>cold</u>, <u>dry</u> winters.

11. <u>The</u> Mediterranean climate has <u>a</u> <u>mild</u>, <u>rainy</u> winter and <u>a</u> <u>hot</u>, <u>dry</u> summer.

12. <u>Luscious</u> <u>citrus</u> fruits, <u>olive</u> trees, and <u>cedar</u> trees grow in <u>this</u> type of <u>temperate</u> zone.

13. <u>The</u> <u>tropical</u> rain forest in <u>the</u> <u>torrid</u> zone is known for <u>its</u> <u>scorching</u> heat, <u>humid</u> atmosphere, <u>tall</u> trees, and <u>heavy</u> vines.

14. <u>Many</u> <u>interesting</u> animals live in <u>the</u> savanna where <u>tall</u>, <u>tough</u> grasses and <u>some</u> trees grow.

15. <u>Mr. Haroon's</u> safari took him to <u>remote</u> places.

16. <u>Few</u> people have visited <u>these</u> regions.

17. <u>His</u> jeep lost <u>its</u> brakes as it thundered down <u>a</u> <u>steep</u>, <u>bumpy</u> road.

18. <u>Several</u> <u>swift</u> gnus with <u>curved</u> horns came to <u>the</u> rescue.

More Practice

Lesson 29

Circle each letter that should be capitalized in these sentences.

1. (d)r. and (m)rs. (n)g attend the (b)aptist church on (e)mmons (d)rive.

2. (i) believe (r)abbi (f)eingold lives in the (n)orthwest.

3. (n)ext (s)aturday we will accompany (m)rs. (y)u to the (a)rcadia (p)ublic (l)ibrary.

4. (w)e find books such as (g)enesis, (e)xodus, (l)eviticus, (n)umbers, and (d)euteronomy in the (o)ld (t)estament part of the (b)ible.

5. (c)atholics, (p)resbyterians, and (e)piscopalians worship (j)esus (c)hrist.

6. (m)r. (y)u, a (b)uddhist, came to this country from the (f)ar (e)ast.

7. (w)e (a)mericans are free to worship in our own way.

8. (a)braham is the forefather of (m)uslims, (j)ews, and (c)hristians.

9. (w)here did (m)oses take the (h)ebrew people?

10. (a)noop reads the (k)oran, the holy book of the (i)slamic faith.

11. (w)hen will (f)ather (o)'(m)alley preach again in the (s)outhwest?

12. (d)r. (m)artin (l)uther (k)ing, (j)r. challenged people all over the country, but especially in the (s)outh.

13. (a)s (w)orld (w)ar II was ending, (r)uth (g)ruber helped thousands of (j)ewish refugees to escape (n)azi terror and make their homes in our country.

14. (w)assim, a (m)uslim, worships (a)llah.

15. (o)f course, (r)abbi (g)olden was reading from the (t)orah.

16. (d)ear (f)reddy,
     (p)lease wait for me after school.
                              (l)ove,
                              (b)eth

Circle every capital letter that does not belong in these sentences.

1. In his Physical Education class, Michael played Water Polo and Football.

2. At the Zoo, I saw an African Rhinoceros and a Hippopotamus.

3. In addition to English Walnuts, Colonel Mustard grows Pecans and Washington Apples.

4. His wife has planted Pansies, Marigolds, and African Violets.

5. Would you like French Vanilla or Dutch Chocolate Ice Cream?

6. Until she caught the German measles, Lana was enrolled in Geometry, Biology, and Astronomy.

7. Beth likes Tamales and Enchiladas, but Freddy prefers Chinese Food.

8. Next Spring, we will plant Cucumbers, Green Beans, and Italian Squash.

9. Our Apricots, Peaches, and Plums ripen in early Summer.

10. In the Fall, our Friends, the Lopezes, will move to the South.

11. During the Winter, the Black Squirrels burrow under the snow.

12. I believe Mr. Zee is recovering from a bad case of Conjunctivitis that he caught from his Gnu.

13. Last Summer, he suffered from Gastroenteritis after eating too much New York Cheese Cake.

14. He has been playing Hide-And-Seek and Ping Pong for entertainment.

15. My Mom made Swiss Cheese sandwiches for lunch and Chocolate Eclairs for dessert.

16. Elspeth found a Japanese Beetle in her Chicken Casserole.

Diagram each sentence in the spaces below.

1. Marie Curie, Albert Einstein, and Galileo Galilei made amazing discoveries.

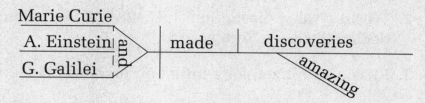

2. Florence Nightengale encouraged and trained other nurses.

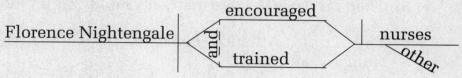

3. She reformed hospitals and nursing schools.

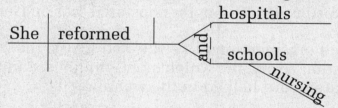

4. She gave hospitals and nurses new ideas.

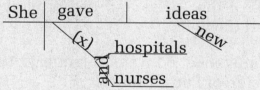

5. Florence Nightengale, tireless and determined, improved the nursing profession.

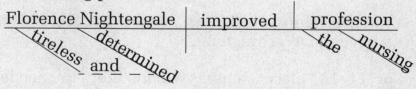

6. Marie and Pierre discovered radium and polonium.

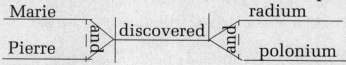

Place commas wherever they are needed in these sentences.

1. On June 28, 1914, a Serbian assassinated the heir to the Austrian throne.

2. World War I began on July 28, 1914, when Austria declared war on Serbia.

3. Russia mobilized for conflict on July 30, 1914.

4. On August 1, 1914, Germany declared war on Russia.

5. Then on August 3, Germany declared war on France.

6. The Triple Alliance consisted of Germany, Austria-Hungary, and Italy.

7. The Triple Entente included Great Britain, France, and Russia.

8. On April 6, 1917, Congress declared war on Germany.

9. Private organizations like the Red Cross, the YMCA, the Salvation Army, the Knights of Columbus, and the Jewish Welfare Board helped in the war effort.

10. On November 11, 1918, in Compiègne, France, representatives of the Allies and of Germany signed an armistice to end the war.

11. The Peace Conference convened January 18, 1919, at Versailles, outside of Paris, France.

12. President Woodrow Wilson collapsed after delivering a speech in Pueblo, Colorado, on September 25, 1919.

13. The White House is located at 1600 Pennsylvania Avenue, Washington, D.C.

For 14–16, place commas where they are needed in these addresses.

14. 11147 Bunbury Street, Saint Louis, Missouri

15. 270 Alta Vista Drive, Tallahassee, Florida

16. 4921 Cedar Avenue, Topeka, Kansas

17. 30 Race Street, Denver, Colorado

Place commas where they are needed in these sentences.

1. Cynthia, please write to me!

2. Father Timothy, rector of an Episcopal church, helps troubled teenagers.

3. Barnabas, his huge black dog, heeds scripture.

4. Are you wearing clean socks, Dooley?

5. I hope, Maggie, that you will leave your iguana at home.

6. Barbra Farris, R.N., worked at a medical clinic in Haiti.

7. Has Dolores Dolorfino, M.D., prescribed antibiotics for your infection?

8. May I wash your car for you, Mr. Rivas?

9. Richard M. Curtis, D.D.S., repaired my broken tooth.

10. I believe Miss Cheung, Vice President, will conduct the next P.T.A. meeting.

11. Gerry Wilson, pastor of the Arcadia Friends Church, led the prayer meeting.

12. Hard-working Pac Couch, District Attorney, won her case in the Supreme Court this morning.

13. Is Mauricio Zelaya, Ph.D., the author of that fine editorial?

14. Judy's restaurant sells pepperoni pizza, my favorite food.

15. The school principal, Mr. Stuart Dunn, gave the students a pep talk.

16. I wish, dear friend, that you lived closer.

17. Anoop Habib, a theologian, studies the Dead Sea Scrolls.

18. The young school board candidate, Andre Quintero, posted hundreds of campaign signs.

19. Mom, can you hear me?

20. I'm happy, Henri, that you came to this country.

Place commas where they are needed.

1. Dear Justin,
   Please dump the trash.
   Love,
   Trevor

2. Hi Trevor,
   I dumped the trash.
   Love,
   Justin

3. Hey Jared,
   I hope you win your soccer game this Saturday.
   Your cousin,
   Mariah

4. The index listed "Revere, Paul" on page 227.

5. He wrote "Hake, Kyle" because it asked for last name first.

6. Sir Isaac Newton, an English mathematician and physicist, brought the scientific revolution of the seventeenth century to its climax.

7. In fact, he established the principal outlines of our system of natural science.

8. In mathematics, he was the first person to develop the calculus.

9. The calculus, a new and powerful instrument, carried modern mathematics above the level of Greek geometry.

10. Newton's three laws of motion, I believe, became the foundation of modern dynamics.

11. From these three laws of motion, he derived the law of universal gravitation.

12. In addition, Newton studied optics and the phenomena of colors.

13. To explain how colors arise, he proved that sunlight is a mixture of different rays that create different colors.

14. Edmund Halley, I understand, visited Isaac Newton in 1684.

15. Among other things, Halley and Newton discussed orbital motion.

16. After this discussion, Newton published his ideas about universal gravitation.

More Practice Lesson 57

Underline the dependent clause in each sentence, and circle the subordinating conjunction.

1. (After) a Viking tribe, the Russes, invaded, the land became known as the Land of the Rus, or Russia.

2. I have heard (that) the city of Kiev became the political and religious center of Russia.

3. (While) the Mongols ruled Russia, the religious center moved from Kiev to Moscow.

4. Ivan III became the first true national leader of Russia (after) the Mongolian troops were defeated.

5. (Because) he enslaved workers, Ivan IV became known as Ivan the Terrible.

6. You may remember (that) other famous czars included Peter the Great, Catherine the Great, and Alexander.

7. (Even though) Russia was already a huge territory, the czars wanted to expand the empire.

8. (While) Nicholas I was czar, Russia added many countries to its empire.

9. (Since) the secret police controlled the press and universities, the government controlled every part of Russian thought and life.

10. Nicholas I crushed a revolt of the Russian people (so that) the central government kept growing stronger.

11. (Although) the French emperor Napoleon marched into Moscow, the cold Russian winter defeated his army.

12. (When) Russian factory workers revolted in 1905, Nicholas II crushed them.

13. (As) World War I ended, conditions were even worse for the Russian people.

14. (While) events were building to a breaking point in Russia, the idea of Marxism arose.

15. The working class could control the government (as soon as) the upper and middle classes were abolished.

16. The government would own all property (so that) everyone would be "equal."

17. (If) Marxists wanted a successful Communist government, they would have to kill entire classes of people.

18. (After) the Bolsheviks overthrew the Russian people's government, Lenin became the leader of the first Communist state in history.

For 1–6, underline each participal phrase and circle the word it modifies.

1. The (sailor), weathered by experience, held the rudder.

2. Having given his opinion, (Oscar) sat down.

3. The (man) driving that truck is my neighbor.

4. Running around the park, (Steve) saw an old friend.

5. Having studied for hours, (Elmo) felt confident about his geometry test.

6. The little (boy) blowing bubbles is my nephew.

For 7–10, complete the diagram of each sentence.

7. His limping deceived us.

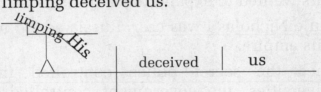

8. Emelina enjoys feeding her pigeons.

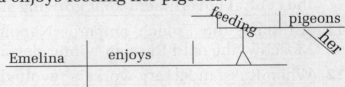

9. Riding a unicycle, Cisco impressed the crowd.

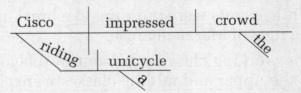

10. Having finished the race, we rested.

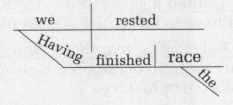

Place commas where they are needed in these sentences.

1. Although the Russian people resisted Lenin's Communism, Lenin forced his power upon them.

2. Since Communists ruled, the government took control of all land and major industries.

3. Food and goods were meagerly distributed by this cruel, tyrannical government.

4. As the government took control, all private trade was stopped.

5. Because the government owned all property, churches were closed or controlled by the government.

6. Though White Russians opposed Communism, they were overcome by the Red Russian Communists.

7. Lenin took away the freedoms of speech, press, and religion.

8. Since human life had no value, many "enemies of the state" were executed.

9. Even though Russia's economy collapsed under Communism, the Communists would not admit their failure.

10. Artists, writers, and musicians were forced to work for the government.

11. After Lenin died, Joseph Stalin became Russia's dictator.

12. When people opposed Stalin, they were killed.

13. While Nikita Krushchev ruled Russia, many Eastern European Nations were taken over by Communists.

14. This oppressive, cruel form of government resulted in poor, starved, uneducated people.

15. If a government oppresses its people, it will eventually crumble.

Place commas where they are needed in these sentences.

1. Benjamin Franklin said, "Content makes poor men rich; discontent makes rich men poor."

2. In *Othello*, William Shakespeare wrote, "Poor and content is rich and rich enough."

3. "The noblest mind the best contentment has," wrote Edmund Spencer in *The Faerie Queen*.

4. "To know what is right and not do it is the worst cowardice," said Confucius.

5. An old French proverb says, "Justifying a fault doubles it."

6. Woodrow Wilson said, "I believe in democracy because it releases the energies of every human being."

7. On December 14, 1799, George Washington spoke his last words, "Doctor, I die hard, but I am not afraid to go."

8. On his deathbed in 1848, John Quincy Adams said, "This is the last of earth! I am content."

9. We can have fear, or we can have faith.

10. He would not forgive, nor would he forget.

11. Unforgiveness embitters the soul, but forgiveness brings life.

12. She asked for forgiveness, for she was sorry.

13. Envy rots the bones, but love heals all wounds.

14. Ben Franklin wrote wise words, so we remember them.

15. "Envy is an enemy of honor," says an old proverb.

16. I believe her testimony, for she has integrity.

17. The fireman was exhausted, yet he continued searching.

18. Referring to the American flag, Charles Sumner said, "White is for purity, red for valor, blue for justice."

Place quotation marks where they are needed in these sentences.

1. Oliver Wendell Holmes said, "Fame usually comes to those who are thinking about something else."

2. "They are able because they think they are able," said Virgil in the *Aeneid*.

3. A Hindu proverb warns, "Even nectar is poison if taken in excess."

4. "It is better to be the enemy of a wise man," said the Hindu sage, "than the friend of a fool."

5. "A wise man will make haste to forgive," said Samuel Johnson, "because he knows the true value of time, and will not suffer it to pass away in unnecessary pain."

6. A Danish proverb says, "There is no need to hang a bell on a fool."

7. "Dig a well before you are thirsty," advised the Chinese scholar.

8. "Life has taught me to forgive," said Otto Von Bismarck, "but to seek forgiveness still more."

9. "Free countries are those in which the rights of man are respected," said Robespierre, "and the laws, in consequence, are just."

10. "Those who deny freedom to others deserve it not for themselves," said Lincoln, "and, under a just God, cannot long retain it."

11. Rudyard Kipling said, "All we have of freedom—all we use or know—This our fathers bought for us, long and long ago."

12. "Freedom exists," said Woodrow Wilson, "only where people take care of the government."

13. Leonardo da Vinci advised, "Reprove a friend in secret, but praise him before others."

14. "A friend should bear his friend's infirmities," wrote Shakespeare.

For 1–16, place quotation marks where they are needed in the dialogs.

We read this dialogue in *The Wizard of Oz* by L. Frank Baum:

1. "Where is the Emerald City?" he inquired. "And who is Oz?"

2. "Why, don't you know?" she returned in surprise.

3. "No, indeed; I don't know anything. You see, I am stuffed, so I have no brains at all," he answered sadly.

4. "Oh," said Dorothy, "I'm awfully sorry for you."

We find this dialogue in *Dr. Jekyll and Mr. Hyde* by Robert Louis Stevenson:

5. "Have you the envelope?" he asked.

6. "I burned it," replied Jekyll, "before I thought what I was about. But it bore no postmark. The note was handed in."

7. "Shall I keep this and sleep upon it?" asked Uterson.

8. "I wish you to judge for me entirely," was the reply. "I have lost confidence in myself."

We read the following dialog in *Johnny Tremain* by Esther Forbes:

9. Cilla said, "You watch him much?"

10. He answered a little miserably, "It's just like I can't help it. I don't mean ever to think of him."

11. Isannah murmured, "What do they do with their pearls?"

12. "They drink their pearls."

This dialog comes from C.S. Lewis's *The Silver Chair*:

13. "Good-bye, dear Puddleglum," said Jill going over to the Marsh-wiggle's bed. "I'm sorry we called you a wet blanket."

14. "So'm I," said Eustace. "You've been the best friend in the world."

15. "And I do hope we'll meet again," added Jill.

16. "Not much chance of that, I should say," replied Puddleglum. "I don't reckon I'm very likely to see my old wigwam either...."   *(cont. next page)

For 17–29, enclose titles of short literary works in quotation marks.

17. Oliver Wendell Holmes's poem, "Old Ironsides," talks about a warship used in the War of 1812.

18. In his sermon entitled "Selfishness," Charles Finney discusses this disease and gives a cure for it.

19. The class laughed heartily at Artemus Ward's two humorous essays, "My Life Story" and "A Business Letter."

20. In Nathaniel Hawthorne's short story, "The Great Carbuncle," eight people with varying motives all seek the precious jewel, but it is a risky business.

21. In the computer magazine, Robert read an interesting article, "How to Create Your Own Website."

22. Today, the *Mud Valley News* published an editorial titled "Educational Experimentation using Guinea Pigs."

23. Edgar Allen Poe's poem titled "Alone" describes how the author differs from other people.

24. Mr. Hake, a mathematician, gave a lecture entitled "The Pythagorean Theorem for Dummies."

25. Washington Irving's article, "A Republic of Prairie Dogs," attributes human qualities and characteristics to these little animals.

26. For his science class, Andrew wrote an essay called "The Undefinable Black Hole."

27. Benito's short story, "Life on the Princeton Levee," gained notoriety on the East Coast.

28. William Shakespeare wrote many longer plays, but he also wrote some short poems such as "Under the Greenwood Tree."

29. Francis Bacon (1561–1626), an English philosopher, scientist, and writer, wrote an essay called "On Revenge."

Underline all words that should be italicized in print.

1. Shall we watch the movie <u>Gone with the Wind</u>, or would you rather see <u>Mary Poppins</u>?

2. "The Dance of the Sugar Plum Fairies" is a song from <u>The Nutcracker</u>.

3. The Zamora Family enjoyed the <u>Phantom of the Opera</u>.

4. Kurt plays and replays his CD entitled <u>Veggie Tunes II</u>.

5. Have you read that enchanting novel, <u>The Hobbit</u>, by J.R.R. Tolkien?

6. The aircraft carrier <u>Enterprise</u> entered the Persian Gulf.

7. We cruised Glacier Bay in Alaska on a ship called <u>The Scandinavian Princess</u>.

8. They saw <u>Mona Lisa</u>, Leonardo da Vinci's famous painting, when they visited the Louvre in Paris.

9. Leonardo da Vinci also painted <u>Lady with an Ermine</u>, which can be seen at the Czartoryski Museum in Cracow, Poland.

10. Years ago, we rode the train, <u>Super Chief</u>, from Los Angeles to Chicago.

11. The university owns a reproduction of Rodin's famous statue, <u>The Thinker</u>.

12. The <u>Statue of Liberty</u> welcomes immigrants to a land of opportunity.

13. In Melville's novel, <u>Moby Dick</u>, the evil Captain Ahab believes that he alone can conquer the white whale.

14. Aunt Isabel reads the <u>Los Angeles Times</u> newspaper every morning.

15. Uncle Gerardo subscribes to a magazine called <u>Country Living</u>.

Complete this irregular verb chart by writing the past and past participle forms of each verb.

	VERB	PAST	PAST PARTICIPLE
1.	beat	beat	(has) beaten
2.	bite	bit	(has) bitten
3.	bring	brought	(has) brought
4.	build	built	(has) built
5.	burst	burst	(has) burst
6.	buy	bought	(has) bought
7.	catch	caught	(has) caught
8.	come	came	(has) come
9.	cost	cost	(has) cost
10.	dive	dove	(has) dived
11.	drag	dragged	(has) dragged
12.	draw	drew	(has) drawn
13.	drown	drowned	(has) drowned
14.	drive	drove	(has) driven
15.	eat	ate	(has) eaten
16.	fall	fell	(has) fallen
17.	feel	felt	(has) felt
18.	fight	fought	(has) fought
19.	flee	fled	(has) fled
20.	flow	flowed	(has) flowed
21.	fly	flew	(has) flown
22.	forsake	forsook	(has) forsaken

Underline the correct verb form for each sentence.

1. Yesterday, Arroyo (beated, <u>beat</u>) Rosemead in cross country.

2. Arroyo has (beat, <u>beaten</u>) Rosemead in every meet this season.

3. Hoover (brang, <u>brought</u>) taquitos to share with his friends.

4. In the past, he has (brung, <u>brought</u>) enough for ten.

5. In the 1950s, the L.E. Dixon Company (builded, <u>built</u>) dams in California and Washington.

6. They have also (builded, <u>built</u>) bridges and tunnels.

7. Sam (buyed, <u>bought</u>) me lunch.

8. He has (buyed, <u>bought</u>) me lunch frequently.

9. Hector (catched, <u>caught</u>) the high, fly ball to center field.

10. By the seventh inning, he had (catched, <u>caught</u>) six fly balls.

11. Martha (comed, <u>came</u>) home at noon.

12. She said she had (came, <u>come</u>) to eat lunch.

13. Last Tuesday, apples (costed, <u>cost</u>) 99¢ a pound.

14. They have (<u>cost</u>, costed) less in the past.

15. Kyla (<u>dove</u>, dived) into the pool to rescue her cat.

16. She has (dove, <u>dived</u>) after that cat twice today.

17. Molly and Andrew (drawed, <u>drew</u>) chalk pictures this morning.

18. They have (drew, <u>drawn</u>) several today.

19. Lorna (drived, <u>drove</u>) through the streets in search of Dijon.

20. Dijon has nearly (drove, <u>driven</u>) Lorna crazy.

21. Humpty Dumpty (falled, <u>fell</u>) off the wall this afternoon.

22. Has he ever (falled, fell, <u>fallen</u>) before?

23. The crows and parrots (fighted, <u>fought</u>) over their territory.

24. They have (fighted, <u>fought</u>) every spring.

25. The jet (flied, <u>flew</u>) above the clouds.

26. Christie had never (flew, <u>flown</u>) so high before.

Complete this irregular verb chart by writing the past and past participle forms of each verb.

	VERB	PAST	PAST PARTICIPLE
1.	give	gave	(has) given
2.	go	went	(has) gone
3.	hang (execute)	hanged	(has) hanged
4.	hang (dangle)	hung	(has) hung
5.	hide	hid	(has) hidden
6.	hold	held	(has) held
7.	lay	laid	(has) laid
8.	lead	led	(has) led
9.	lend	lent	(has) lent
10.	lie (recline)	lay	(has) lain
11.	lie (deceive)	lied	(has) lied
12.	lose	lost	(has) lost
13.	make	made	(has) made
14.	mistake	mistook	(has) mistaken
15.	put	put	(has) put
16.	raise	raised	(has) raised
17.	ride	rode	(has) ridden
18.	rise	rose	(has) risen
19.	run	ran	(has) run
20.	see	saw	(has) seen
21.	sell	sold	(has) sold

Underline the correct verb form for each sentence.

1. Silvia and Helen (given, <u>gave</u>) their time to help younger students.

2. They have (gived, gave, <u>given</u>) many hours this week.

3. Rafa and Marta (gone, <u>went</u>) back to Costa Rica yesterday.

4. Have they (<u>gone</u>, went) already?

5. We (hanged, <u>hung</u>) our clothes in the closet.

6. We have (hanged, <u>hung</u>) them all in the closet.

7. Ernie (hided, <u>hid</u>) behind the sofa.

8. He has (hid, <u>hidden</u>) there before.

9. Kerry (holded, <u>held</u>) the sleeping baby.

10. She has (holded, <u>held</u>) the baby all day.

11. Fatima (layed, <u>laid</u>) the catalog on her desk.

12. She has (layed, <u>laid</u>, lain) it there before.

13. Zack felt exhausted, so he (laid, <u>lay</u>) down for a while.

14. He has (laid, <u>lain</u>) there since noon.

15. Unfortunately, I (losed, <u>lost</u>) my library card.

16. Have you (losed, <u>lost</u>) your also?

17. Emelina (maked, <u>made</u>) pupusas.

18. I thought she had (maked, <u>made</u>) pancakes.

19. One day, she absentmindedly (<u>put</u>, putted) her iron in the refrigerator.

20. Never before had she (<u>put</u>, putted) it there.

21. They (rised, <u>rose</u>) from their seats when the national anthem began.

22. We have always (rose, <u>risen</u>) to salute the flag.

23. They (<u>saw</u>, seen) each other today.

24. They have (saw, <u>seen</u>) each other every day.

25. I believe they have (selled, <u>sold</u>) their home.

Complete this irregular verb chart by writing the past and past participle forms of each verb.

	VERB	PAST	PAST PARTICIPLE
1.	set	set	(has) set
2.	shake	shook	(has) shaken
3.	shine (light)	shone	(has) shone
4.	shine (polish)	shined	(has) shined
5.	shut	shut	(has) shut
6.	sit	sat	(has) sat
7.	slay	slew	(has) slain
8.	sleep	slept	(has) slept
9.	spring	sprang, sprung	(has) sprung
10.	stand	stood	(has) stood
11.	strive	strove	(has) striven
12.	swim	swam	(has) swum
13.	swing	swung	(has) swung
14.	take	took	(has) taken
15.	teach	taught	(has) taught
16.	tell	told	(has) told
17.	think	thought	(has) thought
18.	wake	woke, waked	(has) waked
19.	weave	wove	(has) woven
20.	wring	wrung	(has) wrung
21.	write	wrote	(has) written

Underline the correct verb form for each sentence.

1. Last night, I (setted, <u>set</u>) an alarm for 6 a.m.

2. The night before, I had (setted, <u>set</u>) it for 7 a.m.

3. David (<u>shook</u>, shaked) hands with each guest.

4. He has (shook, shaked, <u>shaken</u>) many hands today.

5. The star (shined, <u>shone</u>) brightly in the night sky.

6. It had (shined, <u>shone</u>) brighter the night before.

7. Mr. Peabody (<u>shined</u>, shone) the silverware before the banquet.

8. He has (<u>shined</u>, shone) that silverware faithfully every month.

9. The Cozaks (shutted, <u>shut</u>) their windows because it was windy.

10. Have they (shutted, <u>shut</u>) the windows to keep out the noise?

11. Myrtle the Turtle (sitten, <u>sat</u>) in the sun.

12. She had (sitted, <u>sat</u>) there for hours before I noticed her.

13. Fong (<u>slept</u>, sleeped) through the tornado.

14. Have you ever (<u>slept</u>, sleeped) through a tornado?

15. The grandfather clock (standed, <u>stood</u>) in a corner.

16. It had (standed, <u>stood</u>) there for a hundred years.

17. The little fish (<u>swam</u>, swum) away from the big fish.

18. Has the little fish ever (swam, <u>swum</u>) alongside a big fish?

19. Has Freddy (took, <u>taken</u>) Turbo and Sophie to the dog groomer?

20. Yes, Freddy (<u>took</u>, taken) them to the groomer yesterday.

21. Blanca (teached, <u>taught</u>) me to make albondigas.

22. She has (teached, <u>taught</u>) me to make several delicious dishes.

23. Has Ilbea (telled, <u>told</u>) you her plans?

24. Yes, she (telled, <u>told</u>) me yesterday.

25. Have you (thinked, <u>thought</u>) about learning a foreign language?

26. Yes, I (thinked, <u>thought</u>) I would study Arabic next year.

Underline each adverb in these sentences.

1. <u>Now</u>, I <u>clearly</u> remember what happened <u>yesterday</u>.

2. It was snowing <u>very</u> <u>hard</u>, so I went <u>out</u> to shovel the driveway.

3. I had <u>not</u> <u>quite</u> finished when the snowplow drove <u>by</u>.

4. <u>Rather</u> <u>rudely</u>, the driver laughed and told me I would be shoveling <u>forever</u>.

5. <u>Completely</u> annoyed, I shoveled <u>more</u> <u>energetically</u> to prove to the driver that I was <u>not</u> a weakling.

6. I tossed snow <u>everywhere</u> and <u>barely</u> felt the cold.

7. My family sat <u>cozily</u> <u>inside</u>; they were <u>quite</u> oblivious to my labor.

8. <u>Soon</u>, I looked <u>around</u> and realized that snow <u>still</u> covered the driveway.

9. <u>Then</u> snow began falling <u>too</u> <u>heavily</u> for me to make any progress.

10. I wouldn<u>'t</u> give <u>up</u>.

11. <u>Highly</u> motivated to maintain my pride, I shoveled <u>frantically</u>.

12. My neighbor shook her head <u>slightly</u> and pointed <u>up</u>.

13. "It is <u>not</u> <u>very</u> smart to shovel snow <u>today</u>," she said <u>simply</u>.

14. <u>Even</u> <u>more</u> determined, I ignored her.

15. I looked <u>down</u> and never glanced <u>up</u>, so I didn't notice the branch that sagged <u>above</u>.

16. It was <u>heavily</u> loaded with snow.

17. It cracked <u>loudly</u>, but the snow fell <u>silently</u>.

18. I was <u>underneath</u>.

Replace commas with semicolons where they are needed in these sentences.

1. Cities with Native American names include Wichita, Kansas; Tucson, Arizona; Tallahassee, Florida; Minneapolis, Minnesota; and Seminole, Oklahoma.

2. The sales representative passes through Denver, Colorado; Austin, Texas; and Memphis, Tennessee.

3. Damien plays drums; Annie plays the saxophone, the flute, and the trumpet.

4. Okra and artichokes are vegetables; tangarines, apricots, and nectarines are fruits.

5. Dr. Hagelganz spoke this week; moreover, Foster Shannon will speak next week.

6. James washed the car, cleaned the house, and mowed the lawn; consequently, he fell asleep during the movie.

7. I like to bake cookies, cakes, and pies; however, I've never made an eclair.

8. In November a pound of bananas cost 29¢; in December, 39¢; in January, 49¢; in February, 59¢; and in March, 69¢.

9. I worked all day; therefore, I finished the project on time.

10. Donald and Tim will be there; also, Cecilia will come if she can.

11. She enjoys planting trees; for example, she planted two oaks and a cedar last fall.

12. Joe cleaned the kitchen; furthermore, he organized all the cupboards and drawers.

13. The weather was cold; nevertheless, Bob hiked to the top of the mountain.

14. He wore his new shoes; as a result, he has blisters on his feet.

15. Would you rather visit Paris, France; Rome, Italy; Juneau, Alaska; or Moscow, Russia?

Insert apostrophes where they are needed in these sentences.

1. She couldn't recall what she'd done during the summers of '68 and '70.

2. I can't remember their address, but I'm sure it has several *7*s.

3. They're playing tic-tac-toe; they're carefully placing their *x*'s and *o*'s.

4. "I've been standin' here waitin' for twenty minutes," he complained.

5. "I'm sorry," she said, "but I didn't see you."

6. Aren't malapropisms funny?

7. Wasn't he born in '48?

8. That's not the only novel we've studied.

9. I think he's a troublemaker, a proponent of dissention.

10. Wouldn't you agree?

11. Perhaps she'll counsel him confidentially.

12. If it's Monday, you'd be smart to elude him entirely.

13. They couldn't see their psychosis from our perspective.

14. They've completed the prototype, and they're ready to try it.

15. We've heard the parable, but we haven't understood its meaning.

16. She's kept her old customs, but she isn't wearing the traditional costume.

17. If you've synchronized your watches, then you're set to begin.

18. "What's that screamin' noise?" asked Authur.

19. "Bill's practicin' the saxophone," Max replied.

20. I don't think it's treason, but I'm sure it's a crime.

For 1–4, complete each sentence diagram.

1. Ancient Greeks admired physical fitness; citizens exercised at the public gymnasium.

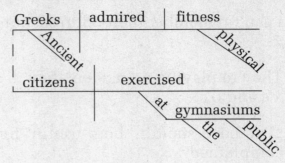

2. Asclepius, who usually carried a snake coiled around his staff, was the Greek god of healing.

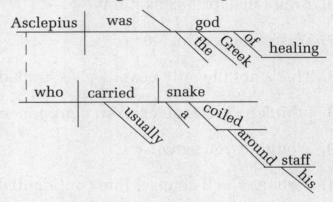

3. Hippocrates carefully observed patients' symptoms before he made a diagnosis.

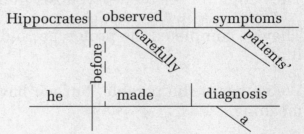

4. Having sworn the Hippocratic oath, Dr. Ngo gave his patients his best effort.

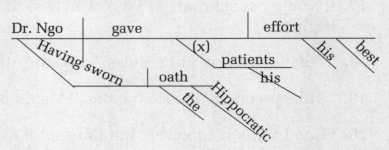

For 5–8, diagram each sentence in the space provided.

5. Developing more successful methods of healing was Hippocrates' goal.

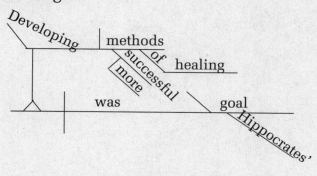

6. Hippocrates, the founder of scientific medicine, practiced and taught on the island of Cos.

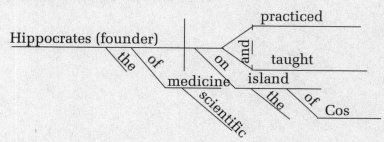

7. After we study the whole system, we can understand the various parts of the body.

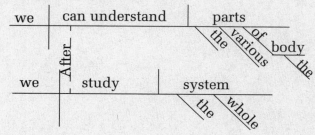

8. The great Pericles died in a plague since the ancient world had no protection against epidemic diseases.

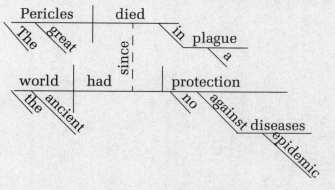

For 1–4, tell whether the sentence is declarative, interrogative, exclamatory, or imperative.

1. Fables were passed down by word of mouth. _____
(1)

2. Do you think that Aesop was creative? _____
(1)

3. Read as much as you can. _____
(1)

4. Watch out! _____
(1)

write the words

5. Circle each letter that should be capitalized in this sentence: On wednesday, mr. wu will plant an
(5) australian willow at santa anita park in california.

In the space to the right, diagram the simple subject and simple predicate of sentences 6 and 7.

6. Did you understand the instructions?
(2, 4)

7. The country mouse loved his home.
(2, 4)

write

For 8–10, circle the best word to complete each sentence.

8. Does the country mouse (adopt, adept, adapt) well to the city?
(1)

9. *Humane* means (ape-like, kind, cruel).
(3)

10. The American flag (waives, waves) from many homes.
(5)

For 11–13, write whether the expression is a sentence fragment, run-on sentence, or complete sentence:

11. A camel dances like a monkey it looks ridiculous. _____
(3)

12. The farmer and his wife prove their impulsiveness. _____
(3)

13. Killing the goose, the source of the golden eggs. _____
(3)

Make a complete sentence from fragments 14 and 15.

14. Has no brains. _____
(3)

15. A fox with a bad attitude. _____
(3)

For 16 and 17, add periods and capital letters to correct the run-on sentences.

16. The fox had a bad attitude he said that the grapes were probably sour.
(3, 5)

17. The gnat made a fool of himself he thought that he was more important than he really was.
(3, 5)

For sentences 18 and 19, circle the action verb.

18. The farmer and his wife slaughtered the goose.
(4)

19. A hawk captured the mouse and the frog.
(4)

20. Replace the verb in the sentence below with one that might be more precise. _____
(4)

The city mouse dislikes the country.

1. In the sentence below, circle each noun and label it *S* for singular or *P* for plural.
(9)

Monkeys laughed at the dancing camel.

2. In the sentence below, circle each noun and label it *F* for feminine, *M* for masculine, *I* for indefinite, or *N*
(9) for neuter.

Like my dog, that doe and that buck have beautiful brown eyes.

3. Circle the compound noun in this sentence: The soapbox derby is next Saturday, February 3.
(9)

4. Circle the possessive noun in this sentence: The basketball player's shoes provided good traction.
(9)

5. Circle the correct verb form for this sentence: She researched the topic and (types, typed) her report.
(6)

6. Replace the blank with the singular present tense form of the verb: Many people <u>floss</u> their teeth daily,
(6) but Ross _____ his teeth twice each day.

7. In the sentence below, circle the verb phrase and label it past, present, or future tense.
(6, 10)

Nancy and Jim will adopt a border collie. _____ tense

8. Circle each helping verb from this list: his   am   car   was   were   tea   being   been   pay   fight
(8)
rust   tan   could   should   would   has   have   mad   to   does   did   shall   fill

In the space to the right, diagram the simple subject and simple predicate of sentences 9 and 10.

9. The police will record your account of the incident.
(2, 4)

10. Set your umbrella on the floor.
(2, 4)

For 11–13, write whether the expression is a complete sentence, sentence fragment, or run-on sentence.

11. We thought we had missed the bus then it appeared. _____
(3)

12. With wisdom and stamina far greater than mine. _____
(3)

13. Approaching American literature with an open mind, we can appreciate its authors. _____
(3)

14. Circle the abstract noun from this sentence: Three men survived the fiery furnace, for they had faith.
(7)

15. Circle the collective noun in this sentence: A herd of cattle grazed in the meadow.
(7)

16. Unscramble these words to make an interrogative sentence.
(1)

you   what   about   do   know   Babylon

_____

17. Circle each letter that should be capitalized in this sentence: After the bombing of pearl harbor, the united
(5) states became an ally of great britain and france in world war II.

Circle the best word to complete sentences 18–20.

18. A microbus is a (large, small, heavy) bus.
(4)

19. The prefix (macro-, micro-, miso-) means hatred.
(7)

20. My good friend is also my (alley, ally).
(8)

1. For a–d, circle the correct verb form.
(14)

    (a) You (am, are, is)   (b) They (am, are, is)   (c) It (do, does)   (d) I (do, does)

For 2–5, write the plural of each singular noun.

2. library _____
(12, 13)

3. alley _____
(12, 13)

4. glass _____
(12, 13)

5. fistful _____
(12, 13)

For sentences 8–10, circle the entire verb phrase and name its tense "past," "present," or "future."

8. During frontier days, people concocted tall tales about heroic cowboys. _____ tense
(6, 10)

9. One of eighteen children, a baby, falls out the back of a covered wagon. _____ tense
(6, 10)

10. A mother coyote will raise this baby. _____ tense
(6, 10)

11. Circle each helping verb in this sentence:
(8)

    Coyotes might have taught Pecos Bill the secrets of survival on the prairie.

12. Underline each noun in this sentence and circle the one that is compound:
(9)

    While playing on the prairie with the antelope and rabbits, Bill meets a man on horseback.

13. Circle each abstract noun from this list: rattlesnake   imagination   cowboy   confidence
(7)

14. Write the present participle, past tense, and past participle of the verb *howl*.
(15)

_____

Circle the correct word to complete sentences 15–17.

15. This sentence is (declarative, imperative, interrogative, exclamatory): Was Pecos Bill a real person?
(1)

16. Although he thought he was a coyote, Pecos Bill was actually (human, humane).
(3)

17. The Greek prefix (micro-, miso-, macro-) means large.
(2)

18. Circle the complete sentence from the word groups below.
(3)

    During a long, hot drought in the state of Texas.

    Jumping on his horse, Widow-Maker, and riding to Oklahoma.

    Pecos Bill lassoes a cyclone.

19. Circle each letter that should be capitalized in the sentence below.
(5, 11)

    yes, i believe he will bring rain back to texas before september.

20. Diagram the simple subject and simple predicate of this sentence:
(2, 4)

    Pecos Bill might have howled like a coyote.

Circle the correct word to complete sentences 1–5.

1. Paul Bunyan was tall in (statue, stature, statute).
(10)

2. The Greek root *mania* means (large, hatred, passion) or madness.
(16)

3. American tall tales (am, is, are) full of humorous exaggerations.
(14)

4. The tall tale hero Paul Bunyan (have, has) a blue ox named Babe.
(14)

5. (Do, Does) Paul really create earthquakes with his hiccups?
(14)

For sentences 6–8, underline the entire verb phrase and complete the name of its tense by adding "present," "past," or "future."

6. Has the logger actually blown birds from Maine to California with his sneeze? _____ perfect
(18) tense

7. According to the tale, the giant baby ox had been shivering in a snowdrift. _____ perfect
(18) progressive tense

8. By the end of the story, Paul will have dug the entire Mississippi River with his shovel. _____
(18) perfect tense

9. Underline each noun in this sentence and circle the one that is collective: My family believes that Paul
(7) Bunyan cut out the Grand Canyon with his ax.

10. Circle each abstract noun in this list: snow   exaggeration   canal   humor   Alaska   heresy
(7)

11. Circle each possessive noun from this list: Babes, Babe's, countries, country's, loggers, loggers'
(9)

For 12 and 13, write the plural of each noun.

12. batch _____   **13.** penny _____
(12, 13)   *(12, 13)*

14. Write the present participle, past tense, and past participle of the verb *exaggerate*.
(15)

_____

15. Circle the gerund in this sentence: Paul Bunyan's fantastic logging provided lumber for homes, schools,
(19) churches, boats, and furniture.

Circle each preposition in sentences 16 and 17.

16. According to the tale, Paul pulled the half-frozen baby ox from under the blue snowdrift and warmed it
(16, 17) in front of the fire.

17. On account of his amazing strength, this hero could cut a hundred trees with one swing of his ax.
(16, 17)

18. Circle each letter that should be capitalized in this sentence: if you visit the state of alaska, you might
(5, 20) still hear the echoes when paul bunyan shouts, "timber!"

In the space to the right, diagram the simple subject and simple predicate of sentences 19 and 20.

19. Blue's shivering had attracted Paul's attention.
(4, 19)

20. Was the snow shivering also?
(2, 4)

Circle the best word(s) to complete sentences 1–6.

1. The mother duck will (sit, set, sat) on the largest egg until it hatches.
(24,)

2. The largest egg (lay, laid, lied) in the nest after all the others had hatched.
(23)

3. That little duck (have, has) finally broken out of the shell.
(14)

4. (Do, Does) he look like the other ducklings?
(14)

5. This sentence is (declarative, interrogative, imperative, exclamatory): Look! That's life!
(1)

6. The following is a (sentence fragment, run-on sentence, complete sentence): The ugly, gray duckling
(3) swam.

For 7 and 8, write the plural form of each singular noun.

7. Jenny _____   **8.** woman _____
(9)   (12, 13)

9. Circle each letter that should be capitalized in this sentence: in hans christian andersen's "the ugly
(5, 20) duckling," a little duck says, "i am so ugly that the dog won't even bite me!"

10. Circle each preposition from this sentence: The ugly, gray duckling swam around the pond, behind the
(16, 17) mother duck, alongside of the other ducklings.

For sentences 11–14, underline the entire verb phrase and complete the name of its tense by adding "past," "present," or "future."

11. The ugly duckling has developed a complex about his appearance. _____ perfect tense
(18)

12. By the end of the fairy tale, he will have transformed into a beautiful swan. _____ perfect
(18) tense

13. He will be rejoicing after the hard winter. _____ progressive tense
(21)

14. In the spring, the duckling had been traveling for many miles. _____ perfect progressive
(21) tense

15. From the sentence below, underline each concrete noun and circle the one that is abstract.
(7)
                    The ugly duckling suffered persecution from the other ducks in the pond.

16. Circle the gerund in this sentence: Flapping its wings brought freedom to the ugly duckling.
(19)

17. Circle the infinitive in this sentence: To persecute the less fortunate seems cruel.
(23)

For 18 and 19, circle to indicate whether the expression is a phrase or a clause.

18. from a clumsy, dark-gray bird to a beautiful swan   (phrase, clause)
(24)

19. before the duckling discovered his transformation   (phrase, clause)
(24)

20. In the space to the right, diagram the simple
(23, 25) subject, simple predicate, and direct object of this
         sentence: The swan has been learning to fly.

Circle the best word(s) to complete sentences 1–9.

1. The Greek prefix *megalo-* means (madness, small, large).
(17)

2. Did (there, their, they're) dog bark all night?
(19)

3. The (progressive, perfect) verb tense shows action that has been completed.
(18, 21)

4. The most commonly used adjectives, and the shortest, are the (articles, pronouns) *a, an,* and *the.*
(28)

5. Examples of (possessive, descriptive) adjectives are *his, her, their, your, its, our,* and *my.*
(28)

6. The sentence below is (declarative, imperative, interrogative, exclamatory):
(1)

Hey, my sweet peas have disappeared!

7. The word group below is a (sentence fragment, run-on sentence, complete sentence):
(3)

A large, well-kept garden on the outskirts of the city.

8. This word group is a (phrase, clause): when summer comes again
(24)

9. The sentence below contains an (action, linking) verb.
(4, 22)

The rabbit felt fearful of my basset hound, Max.

For 10 and 11, write the plural form of each noun.

10. wife _____   **11.** party _____
(12, 13)   *(12, 13)*

For 12 and 13, circle each letter that should be capitalized.

12. the gardener explained, "i have been chasing that rabbit all over flora street."
(5, 20)

13. dear professor hatti,
(5, 29)   there are many different religions in the west....
sincerely,
faith

14. Circle each preposition in this sentence: The old rabbit from this fairytale lives in a dark pit along with
(16, 17) twenty white elephants.

15. Circle the abstract noun from this list: gardener, slugs, flowers, peace, vegetables, rabbit
(7)

16. Circle the gerund from this sentence: My dog, Max, enjoys digging.
(19)

17. Circle the infinitive from this sentence: At night, he likes to howl.
(23)

18. For a–c, circle the correct irregular verb form.
(14)   (a) They (has, have)   (b) I (am, is, are)   (c) He (do, does)

19. In the sentence below, circle the verb phrase and name its tense.
(21)

Max is fighting the ferocious old rabbit.   _____ tense

20. In the space to the right, diagram each word of this
(19, 27) sentence: My intelligent cousin enjoys reading.

Circle the correct word to complete sentences 1–6.

1. A prefix meaning "with" or "together" is (phobia-, syn-, peri-).
(35)

2. A prefix meaning "around," "about," or "surrounding" is (miso-, eu-, peri-).
(25)

3. This sentence is (declarative, imperative, interrogative, exclamatory): Run as fast as you can.
(1)

4. The word group below is a (sentence fragment, run-on sentence, complete sentence).
(3)
     Uncle Remus told a story to a little seven-year-old boy he was the son of Miss Sally.

5. This word group is a (phrase, clause): because Brer Fox wanted to capture Brer Rabbit
(24)

6. The noun or pronoun that follows a preposition is called the (subject, object, modifier) of the preposition.
(32)

7. Circle the concrete noun from this list: Italian, Japanese, Islam, philosophy, rabbit, kindness, stealth
(7)

8. Circle the gerund from this sentence: Swimming is healthful exercise.
(19)

9. Write the plural of the noun *spy*. _____
(12, 13)

10. Circle each letter that should be capitalized in this sentence:
(20, 26) last tuesday, mother and i read, from the story "uncle remus," a rhyme that began, "de place wharbouts you spill de grease…."

11. Circle the four prepositions from this sentence:
(16, 17) Owing to Brer Rabbit's skeptical nature, he successfully escaped from Brer Fox's cave to the closest bush near his rabbit hole.

12. Underline the prepositional phrase and circle the object of the preposition in this sentence: Brer Rabbit
(17, 32) pulled a calamus root out of his dish.

13. Add periods where they are needed in this sentence: Mrs. Wang starts work at Pilgrim Ltd. every day at
(35) eight a.m. sharp.

14. Circle the word from this list that is *not* a helping verb: is, am, are, was, were, be, being, been, has, had,
(8) have, do, does, did, shall, will, smell, should, would, can, could, may, might, must

15. Circle the linking verb in this sentence: The rabbit appears intelligent, for he cleverly outsmarts the fox.
(22)

16. For a–c, circle the correct irregular verb form.
(14) (a) we (was, were)   (b) it (do, does)   (c) you (has, have)

For sentences 17 and 18, underline the verb and circle the direct object if there is one. Then underline "transitive" or "intransitive." (Hint: A "transitive" verb has a direct object.)

17. Brer Rabbit will outsmart Brer Fox time and time again. (transitive, intransitive)
(25, 31)

18. Brer Fox will wait along the path for Brer Rabbit. (transitive, intransitive)
(25, 31)

19. Circle the indirect object in this sentence: Brer Rabbit presents Brer Fox a delicious dinner.
(34)

20. Fill in the blank diagram to the right using
(32, 24) each word of this sentence: Uncle Remus told
the child an amusing story about Brer Rabbit.

Circle the correct word to complete sentences 1–7.

1. The prefix (ante-, caco-, eu-) means before.
(31)

2. The prefix (peri-, tele-, an-) means far or distant.
(28)

3. This sentence is (declarative, imperative, interrogative, exclamatory): Have the sheep been sheared?
(1)

4. This word group is a (sentence fragment, run-on sentence, complete sentence): Clutch was greedy, his
(3) brother would have shared his last morsel with a hungry dog.

5. This word group is a (phrase, clause): until I see you
(24)

6. Coordinating (conjunctions, verbs, nouns) join parts of a sentence that are equal.
(36)

7. Correlative (nouns, adjectives, conjunctions) always come in pairs.
(38)

8. Write the plural of *piccolo*. _____
(12, 13)

9. Write the correct verb form: The brother _____ (present tense of *pity*) Clutch's sheep.
(6)

10. Circle each letter that should be capitalized in this sentence: the teacher required each student to read ray
(5, 20) bradbury's *the martian chronicles*.

11. Underline each prepositional phrase from this sentence and circle the object of each preposition: Away
(17, 32) from their fields, Clutch and his brother, Kind, discover a pasture of violets among the grass.

12. Circle the word from this list that is *not* a helping verb: is, am, are, was, were, be, being, been, here, has,
(8) have, had, may, might, must, can, could, do, does, did, shall, will, should, would

13 Circle each coordinating conjunction from this list: and, but, yet, in, or, on, nor, for, so, do, did, rag
(36)

14. Circle the correlative conjunctions in this sentence: Not only the father but also the son lovingly sheared
(38) the sheep.

15. Circle the gerund in this sentence: The energetic flight attendant likes traveling.
(19)

16. In this sentence, circle the verb phrase and name its tense: Kind has sheared the wolves!
(18) _____ tense

17. Circle the linking verb in this sentence: Caleb hiked all day, but at dusk he grew weary.
(22)

18. Add periods where they are needed in this sentence:
(35)
          Mr. R. U. Greedy, Jr., has been counting money since three a.m.

Complete the diagrams of sentences 19 and 20.

19. The father gave the young shepherds good advice.
(28, 34)

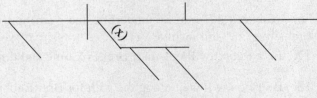

20. The wool of sheep and wolves provides not only
(32, 38) warmth but also protection.

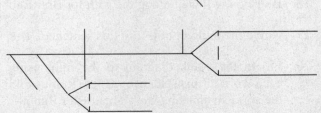

Circle the correct word(s) to complete sentences 1–5.

1. The prefix (*hypo-, hyper-, miso-*) means excessive.
(41)

2. The prefix (*hetero-, homo-*) means different.
(44)

3. The following is a (sentence fragment, run-on sentence, complete sentence): Please listen to me.
(3)

4. This word group is a (phrase, clause): along with an eagle on top of a snow-covered mountain
(24)

5. Of the four Hake brothers, Bryon is the (older, oldest).
(42)

6. Circle the abstract noun from this list: Hinduism, United Kingdom, toenail, Professor Green
(7)

Circle each letter that should be capitalized in 7 and 8.

7. last june, i read an interesting short story called "a seller of dreams."
(11, 20)

8. dear miss stewart,
(26, 29)   did you know that there are many lutherans in the northeast?

                                    warmly,
                                    mallory

9. The plural of the noun *suffix* is _____.
(12, 13)

10. Add commas and periods as needed to this sentence: Mrs. Crabtree promised to bring lettuce, tomatoes,
(35, 44) and cucumbers for our luncheon on Sunday, May 12.

11. Circle the verb phrase in this sentence and label its tense: Peter will be going to his aunt's house.
(21) _____ tense

12. For sentences a and b, circle the verb phrase and then circle action or linking.
(4, 22)
    (a) Does her voice sound sweet and melodious? (action, linking

    (b) Has someone sounded a noisy alarm? (action, linking)

13. Circle the two possessive adjectives in this sentence: After the old seller's warning, Peter's intent was to
(28) rescue Aunt Jane.

14. Circle the correlative conjunctions in this sentence: Not only the guests but also Peter fled the castle.
(38)

15. Circle the predicate nominative in this sentence: The castle became a black shadow.
(39)

For 16–18, write whether the italicized noun is nominative, objective, or possessive case.

16. The man in golden shoes and a scarlet robe is the old *seller* of dreams. _____ case
(40)

17. The ancient castle lies under a terrible *enchantment*. _____ case
(40)

18. Does *Peter's* frightening dream become a reality? _____ case
(40)

Complete the diagrams of sentences 19 and 20.

19. Her nephew, Peter, has a dream about an
(33, 45) enchanted castle.

20. His scary dream becomes significant and
(28, 41) meaningful.

Circle the correct word(s) to complete sentences 1–6.

1. The prefix (pro-, re-, an-) means "before."
(30)

2. The prefix *hetero-* means (same, different).
(44)

3. The past participle of the verb *glare* is (glared, glaring).
(15)

4. The following is a (complete sentence, run-on sentence, sentence fragment):
(3)

I read a poem it was written by Robert Frost.

5. Of the two stories, William Faulkner's is the (more, most) interesting.
(43)

6. (Do, Does) our country have many allies in the fight against terrorism?
(14)

7. Circle each coordinating conjunction in this sentence: We walked, but she drove, so she arrived sooner.
(36)

8. Circle each gerund in this sentence: Theater students usually practice singing, dancing, and acting.
(18)

9. Write the plural of the noun *peach.* _____
(12, 13)

10. Circle the appositive in this sentence: In an old, Anglo-Saxon epic poem, a Scandinavian prince, Beowulf,
(45) rids the Danes of a dreaded monster.

11. Circle each letter that should be capitalized in this sentence: with his family, robert frost sailed across the
(5, 29) atlantic ocean to england.

12. Circle the infinitive in this sentence: Unfortunately, the sea lions refused to perform in front of the crowd.
(23, 48)

13. Underline each prepositional phrase circling the object of each preposition in this sentence: From among
(17, 32) many talented American poets, Robert Frost is the most admired poet of the twentieth century.

14. In the following sentence, circle the verb phrase and name its tense: Fortunately, the antidote has
(18) counteracted the effects of the poison. _____ tense

15. For sentences a and b, circle the verb phrase and then circle transitive or intransitive.
(21, 31)
   (a) The prolific poet has been writing several hundred poems each year. (transitive, intransitive)

   (b) The prolific poet has been writing throughout the entire night. (transitive, intransitive)

16. Circle the sentence below that is written correctly.
(47)

     He likes that kind of a novel.   He likes that kind of novel.

17. Add periods and commas as needed in this sentence: Mrs. May B. Smart teaches violin lessons on
(35) Mondays, Wednesdays, Fridays, and Saturdays.

18. Tell whether the italicized word in this sentence is nominative, objective, or possessive case: The 1930s
(40) brought one *tragedy* after another for Robert Frost. _____ case

19. Underline the pronouns and circle their antecedent in this sentence: Robert Frost lost his youngest
(49) daughter in 1934, his wife in 1938, and his son in 1940.

20. Complete the diagram of this sentence:
(39, 48) Robert Frost is the poet to read.

Circle the best word(s) to complete sentences 1–5.

1. The expression, "the tongue is a fire," is a (pathos, caricature, figure of speech).
(54)

2. The Greek root *anthropos* means (loving, angled, human).
(53)

3. Of the two poems, this one by Langston Hughes is the (good, better, best).
(43)

4. The man on the phone was (he, him).   **5.** Racial prejudice mattered to (he, him)
(53, 54)   (53, 54)

6. Underline each prepositional phrase and circle the object of each preposition in this sentence:
(16, 32)
    In one of his poems, he reflects on blacks being sold down the river into slavery.

7. Circle the verb phrase in this sentence, and then circle transitive or intransitive:
(31)
Did Langston Hughes respond with surprise at his class's choice of him as the class poet? (transitive, intransitive)

8. Write the (a) past tense and (b) past participle of the irregular verb *shrink*.
(15, 52)

    (a)_____   (b) _____

9. Add commas and periods as needed in this sentence:
(35, 46)
    Ernest's father, Dr. Clarence Hemingway, gave Ernest a fishing pole, a net, and new boots.

10. Circle the coordinating conjunction in this sentence: Langston Hughes was a playwright, a novelist, a
(36) song lyricist, and a poet.

11. In this sentence, circle the pronoun and name its case: Unfortunately, she seems as personable as a marble
(53) statue. _____ case

12. Write the plural of the noun *eulogy*. _____
(12, 13)

13. Circle each third person plural pronoun from this list: he, him, she, her, they, them, we, us, you
(51)

14. Circle each objective case pronoun from this list: me, him, I, she, them, they, he, her, we, us
(54)

15. Circle each letter that should be capitalized in this sentence: yes, i believe that langston hughes wrote a
(5, 20) poem titled "the negro speaks of rivers."

16. Circle the verb phrase in this sentence and name its tense: Was that elephant winking at you and me?
(21) _____ tense

17. Circle the infinitive in this sentence: I think it is time to discuss figures of speech.
(23, 48)

18. Circle each possessive noun from this list: person's, persons, bosses, boss's, bosses'
(9, 56)

19. Write the second person singular or plural personal pronoun. _____
(51)

20. Diagram this sentence: Editing and translating
(19, 33) interested this man of many passions.

Circle the correct words to complete sentences 1–9.

1. The prefix *poly-* means (shape, angle, many).   **2.** The Greek word *pseudo* means (real, pretend, love).
(57)   (60)

3. The following word group is a (phrase, clause): Eugene O'Neill, America's first great playwright
(24)

4. Of Eugene O'Neill's many plays, I think *The Iceman Cometh*. is the (more, most) captivating.
(43)

5. A predicate (adjective, nominative, preposition) follows a linking verb and describes the subject.
(41)

6. Unfortunately, the wandering beagle has lost (it's, its) collar.
(56)

7. His brother and (him, he) worked on plays together.
(53, 54)

8. The italicized words in this sentence are (participles, gerunds): The *barking* beagle disturbed my *sleeping*
(58) sister.

9. Have you (spoke, spoken) to your best friend today?
(52)

10. Write the plural of *ally*. _____
(12, 13)

11. Circle the entire verb phrase in this sentence and name its tense: Riveted to the story, Jed had been
(21) reading for three hours. _____ tense

12. Add periods and commas as needed in this sentence and circle each letter that should be capitalized: no,
(5, 35) mr wang, i have never run a marathon. twenty-six miles is too far.

13. Circle the appositive in this sentence: Benjamin Franklin, a brilliant statesman, helped to create the
(45) Constitution of the United States of America.

14. Circle the infinitive in this sentence: After three hours of reading the textbook, Jed began to snore.
(23)

15. Underline the dependent clause and circle the subordinating conjunction in this sentence: Even though
(57) Eugene O'Neill was a successful playwright, his personal life was unhappy.

16. Circle each objective case personal pronoun from this list:
(54)
                me   him   I   she   them   they   he   her   we   us

17. Circle the gerund phrase in this sentence: Following the recipe, Stacy tried cooking a new Chinese dish.
(58)

18. Underline each prepositional phrase and circle the object of each preposition in this sentence: On account
(16, 32) of the drought, water use in our county is restricted during the hot part of the day,

Diagram sentences 19 and 20 in the space to the right.

19. Bursting with creative energy, Eugene O'Neill
(25, 59) wrote many plays.

20. I would like more time to read.
(28, 48)

Circle the correct words to complete sentences 1–10.

1. In the last battle, the victory will be (our's, ours).   **2.** Sue's sister and (her, she) will travel together.
(56)   (53, 54)

3. (Connotation, Denotation) is the literal, or dictionary, meaning.
(61)

4. The Greek root (mania, morphe, biblion) means book.
(64)

5. The following word group is a (phrase, clause): as she carried the heavy pitchers to the soldiers
(24)

6. Of the two newspaper articles, this one is the (more, most) accurate.
(43)

7. A (subordinating, coordinating) conjunction introduces a dependent clause.
(57)

8. The italicized words in this sentence are (participles, gerunds): Benito likes *singing* and *dancing*.
(58)

9. Have you (chose, chosen) your friends wisely?
(52)

10. Augustina, Mary Ambree, and Molly Pitcher took it upon (theirselves, themselves) to fight for their
(60) countries.

11. Write the plural of *fistful*. _____
(9)

12. In the blank, write the correct verb form: Penelope _____ her sister's clothes all
(18) week.   present perfect tense of *wear*

13. Add periods and commas as needed in this sentence and circle each letter that should be capitalized: yes,
(11, 20) i heard dr. chew say, "you need to drink more water, lose some weight, and eat a variety of fruits and
vegetables."

14. Underline the dependent clause and circle the subordinating conjunction in this sentence: Molly Pitcher
(57) fired her husband's cannon until the British were defeated.

15. Circle each adjective in this sentence: The day after the furious battle of Monmouth, a sad-faced widow
(27, 28) had swollen eyes.

16. Circle the appositive in this sentence: Molly Pitcher, a brave volunteer, received a sergeant's commission
(45) and half-pay for life.

17. Circle each nominative case personal pronoun from this list:
(53)
          me   him   I   she   them   they   he   her   we   us

18. Underline the participial phrase in this sentence and circle the word it modifies: That noisy, two-engine
(59) airplane circling the mountain peak disturbed the peaceful slumber of the campers in the forest.

Diagram sentences 19 and 20 in the space to the right.

19. The neighbor who gave me the squash likes
(59, 64) growing vegetables.

20. She prepares the soil, and her husband plants the
(4, 62) seeds.

Circle the correct word to complete sentences 1–10.

1. (Who's, Whose) novel is this?
(64)

2. Joe's dad and (him, he) went hiking.
(53, 54)

3. (Who, Whom) are you calling?
(64)

4. Kate swims faster than (me, I).
(53, 54)

5. The Greek root (*biblion, mania, metron*) means measure.
(67)

6. The Greek root *chroma* means (large, sound, color).
(69)

7. The following word group is a (phrase, clause): a description of the miserable conditions in migrant labor
(24) camps

8. Of the two automobiles, this one is the (more, most) reliable.
(43)

9. The neighbors' house, (which, that) sold yesterday, has two small bedrooms and a large swimming pool.
(64)

10. John Steinbeck and his wife typed and edited the novels (theirselves, themselves).
(60)

11. Write the plural of *dish*. _____
(12, 13)

12. In the blank, write the correct verb form: Carolyn _____ wool from her sheep in
(21) order to make yarn for a blanket.   present progressive tense of *spin*

13. Add periods and commas as needed in this sentence and circle each letter that should be capitalized:
(20, 35) yesterday, john explained, "keyboards, mice, printers, and monitors are all peripherals of computers."

14. Underline the dependent clause and circle the subordinating conjunction in this sentence: *The Grapes of*
(57) *Wrath* is required reading in many schools since it is regarded as an American classic.

15. Add quotation marks as needed in this sentence: Software, said John, is made up of instructions that tell a
(68, 69) computer what to do.

16. Circle the appositive in this sentence: *The Grapes of Wrath*, an influential book, leaves its mark on
(45) generation after generation.

17. Circle the gerund phrase in this sentence: Unfortunately, missing the train caused me to miss my flight
(58) home from Germany.

18. Underline the participial phrase in this sentence and circle the word it modifies: The weary traveler
(59) standing in the rain has been waiting seven hours for a bus to the train station.

Diagram sentences 19 and 20 in the space to the right.

19. Have you read the last chapter of the book?
(28, 33)

20. Carol and he will give Ed and her a tour of Pacific
(34, 37) Grove in California.

Circle the correct word(s) to complete sentences 1–10.

1. The Greek word *derma* means (god, same, skin).
(71)

2. A (stereotype, pun, satire) is a play on words.
(72)

3. (Who, Whom) were you expecting?
(64)

4. I ate more zuccchini than (him, he).
(53, 66)

5. Mom and (I, me) shall visit our elderly friends at the convalescent hospital.
(53, 54)

6. Because of the storm, (we, us) passengers felt turbulence throughout the flight.
(53, 56)

7. The underlined clause in the following sentence is (essential, nonessential): The book that some readers
(65) like best is Edith Wharton's *Age of Innocence*.

8. The book, (which, that) can be found in the fiction section, costs $15.95.
(65)

9. Last summer, I (builded, built) a magnificent sand castle at the beach.
(75)

10. Each of the ladies (want, wants) (their, her) own dog to win the herding contest.
(56, 71)

11. Write the plural of *entry*. _____
(12, 13)

12. In the blank, write the correct verb form: Carolyn _____ her pet emu to the
(18) country fair.   past perfect tense of *bring*

13. Add periods and commas as needed in this sentence and circle each letter that should be capitalized: we
(5, 35) think that mr. crockett, a fellow traveler, may have accidentally picked up tom's suitcase at the train
station in london, england.

14. Underline the dependent clause and circle the subordinating conjunction in this sentence: I read Edith
(57) Wharton's *Ethan Frome* because my teacher recommended it.

15. Add quotation marks as needed in this sentence: Character is doing the right thing when no one is looking,
(68, 69) said Congressman J.C. Watts.

16. Underline each word that should be italicized in this sentence: I read her first poems in a magazine called
(72) The Atlantic Monthly.

17. Circle the gerund phrase in this sentence: Following my neighbor's excellent directions enabled me to
(58) find my way to your house.

18. Underline the participial phrase in this sentence and circle the word it modifies: Having bitten into a sour
(59) peach, Homer grimaced.

Diagram sentences 19 and 20 in the space to the right.

19. Neither of the gentlemen knows his itinerary.
(33, 71)

20. Agnes and she brought me some fresh lemons.
(34, 37)

Circle the correct word(s) to complete sentences 1–10.

1. The Greek root *therap* means (heat, fire, cure).
(79)

2. Hope is the (antithesis, synonym) of despair.
(78)

3. Neither of the students (know, knows) the rules.
(77, 78)

4. I grew more tomatoes than (they, them).
(53, 66)

5. (Me and Dad, Dad and me, Dad and I) will meet you and (she, her) at the natural history museum.
(53, 54)

6. Fern, would you please invite (we, us) goslings to Wilbur's birthday party?
(56, 60)

7. The underlined clause in the following sentence is (essential, nonessential): *Charlotte's Web*, <u>which is a children's story</u>, tells about a kindly spider and a doomed pig, Wilbur the runt.
(65)

8. Wilbur has (lied, lay, lain) on that straw all morning.
(75)

9. One of the pilots (fly, flies) (their, his/her) own plane around the world each spring.
(80)

10. The spider (that, which) counsels Wilbur is named Charlotte.
(65)

11. Write the plural of *self.* _____
(60)

12. In the blank, write the correct verb form: E. B. White _____ some magnificent stories about farm life and its animals.
(18)   present perfect tense of *write*

13. Add punctuation marks as needed in the following and circle each letter that should be capitalized:
(20, 44) *charlotte's web* is about friendship, affection, protection, and adventure. have you read it?

14. Underline the dependent clause and circle the subordinating conjunction in this sentence: The author
(57) provides local color as he describes animals, insects, sights, and sounds on the farm.

15. Add quotation marks as needed in this sentence: Mrs. Poovey has written a delightful essay titled
(68, 69) Crawling Critters on the Bank of Coot's Creek.

16. Underline each word that should be italicized in this sentence: The French say that E. B. White's essays
(72) are très bien.

17. Circle the two gerund phrases in this sentence: Spinning fancy, miraculous webs is Charlotte's way of
(58) communicating with her friends.

18. Underline the participial phrase in this sentence and circle the word it modifies: Cradling the pig in her
(59) arms, Fern feeds Wilbur with a baby bottle.

Diagram sentences 19 and 20 in the space to the right.

19. The heroine of the story is Charlotte, a spider in the
(33, 45) barn.

20. The stories of E. B. White feature talking animals
(33, 48) with human feelings.

Circle the correct word(s) to complete sentences 1–10.

1. The Greek root (*therap-, cosmos, thermo*s) means "heat." **2.** *Psyche* refers to one's (eyes, body, mind).
(85)   (83)

3. He (don't, doesn't) have (no, any) regrets. **4.** We have more earthworms than (they, them).
(14, 81)   (66)

5. (Me and Mom, Mom and me, Mom and I) might see you and (him, he) at the theater.
(53, 54)

6. (Us, We) drama students are studying our parts for the play.
(65)

7. The underlined clause in the following sentence is (essential, nonessential): *Pilgrim*, <u>which is coming</u>
(65) <u>soon to the theater</u>, will capture the attention of people of all ages.

8. Tennessee Williams (drew, drawn) recognition as a playwright during the 1940s and 1950s.
(73)

9. (Do, Does) one of your relatives have (their, his/her) office in Tennessee?
(77, 80)

10. I haven't (ever, never) (saw, seen) Tennessee Williams's *The Glass Menagerie* performed on stage.
(81)

11. Write the plural of *allegory*. _____
(12, 13)

12. In the blank, write the correct verb form: The author _____ much realism into
(18) the story.   present perfect tense of *weave*

For 13 and 14, add quotation marks and punctuation marks as needed. Also, circle each letter that should be capitalized.

13. "i knew from his accent that tennessee williams came from the south," said mrs. poovey.
(29, 68)

14. "before i go to the theater," said mr. poovey, "i must purchase the tickets, wash the car, and mend my torn
(68, 69) tuxedo."

15. Underline the dependent clause and circle the subordinating conjunction in this sentence: Since it takes
(57) place in an existing district of New Orleans, *A Street Car Named Desire* contains realism.

16. Underline each word that should be italicized in this sentence: Tennessee Williams sold his first story,
(72) "The Vengeance of Nitocris," to Weird Tales, a widely circulated magazine.

17. Circle the gerund phrase in this sentence: Having received a typewriter for his eleventh birthday, Stuart
(58) stopped writing longhand.

18. Underline the participial phrase in this sentence and circle the word it modifies: Having received a
(59) computer for his twenty-first birthday, Stuart stopped using the typewriter.

Diagram sentences 19 and 20 in the space to the right.

19. Writing an effective drama may take many years.
(25, 59)

20. Stuart quickly typed his story about pandemonium
(35, 83) behind the stage.

Circle the correct word(s) to complete sentences 1–10.

1. The Greek root *osteo* means (form, world, bone).
(89)

2. Psychology studies the (earth, mind, universe).
(83)

3. She (don't, doesn't) want (no, any) help.
(81)

4. She (isn't, ain't, aren't) as tall as (me, I).
(66, 80)

5. (Me and you, You and me, You and I) shall meet Rob and (he, him) at the library.
(53, 54)

6. The word *not* is an (adjective, adverb, appositive).
(89)

7. The underlined part of this sentence is a(n) (essential, nonessential) part: In the fresco, the man <u>who is</u>
(65) <u>holding a mackerel</u> is a Cretan fisherman.

8. Hector plays basketball (good, well). He plays a (good, well) game of basketball.
(84)

9. The Minoan civilization, on the island of Crete, had (it's, its) own script, called *Linear A*.
(56)

10. I haven't (ever, never) (saw, seen) the island of Crete.
(81)

11. Write the comparative form of the adverb *peacefully.* _____
(90)

12. In the blank, write the correct verb form: Archaeologists _____ for large jars that
(21) once held grain or olive oil in the palace.   present progressive tense of *search*

For 13 and 14, add quotation marks and punctuation marks as needed, circle each letter that should be capitalized, and underline each part that should be italicized.

13. professor minos asked me do you remember from your reading in barker's world history what major crops
(68, 72) the minoans raised

14. yes professor minos i answered the major crops were wheat barley vegetables grapes and olives
(11, 68)

15. Underline the dependent clause and circle the subordinating conjunction in this sentence: We shall sail to
(57) the island of Crete as soon as everyone has boarded the ship.

16. Add hyphens where they are needed in this sentence: Twenty-two plus twenty-one equals forty-three.
(85, 87)

17. Circle the gerund phrase in this sentence: The archeologist purchased a new shovel for digging the ancient
(58) ruins.

18. Underline the participial phrase in this sentence and circle the word it modifies: Digging around ancient
(59) Minoan palaces, archaeologists have uncovered old thrones and decorations.

Diagram sentences 19 and 20 in the space to the right.

19. The Minoans, whom I studied, designed highly
(64, 89) efficient plumbing for their palaces.

20. An erupting volcano seriously threatened the
(33, 48) inhabitants of the island.

Circle the correct word(s) to complete sentences 1–10.

1. The word *sure* is an (adjective, adverb).
(89, 92)

2. The word *really* is an (adjective, adverb).
(89, 92)

3. A hexapod has (four, five, six) legs.
(92)

4. Is Ishani feeling (well, good) today?
(84)

5. The Greek prefix *deka-* means (bad, not, ten).
(94)

6. Can't (nobody, anybody) decipher the script used by the Harappa people in India?
(81)

7. (Beside, Besides) growing vegetables and grains, the Harappas might have been the first people to grow
(95) cotton.

8. The italicized word in this sentence is an (adjective, adverb): We're studying *early* civilizations.
(27, 88)

9. The italicized word in this sentence is an (adjective, adverb): We arrived *early* to hear the lecture.
(27, 88)

10. Maribel hasn't (ever, never) (saw, seen) the Indus Valley where the Harappas lived long ago.
(81)

11. Write the superlative form of the adverb *artfully.* _____
(90)

12. Circle the conjunctive adverb in this sentence: The Harappas had no modern plumbing; however, they
(91) created brick lavatories connected by chutes to a main drain.

For 13 and 14, circle each letter that should be capitalized, and add punctuation marks as needed.

13. professor trinh wrote an article called solving the harappa mystery for he had dug among the ruins along
(50, 69) with a team of archeologists from boston massachusetts.

14. we have found harappa pottery in mesopotamia said professor trinh so we know that these people traded
(30, 68) their goods

15. Insert a colon where it is needed in this sentence: The Harappa farmers grew the following crops: cotton,
(93) wheat, barley, and vegetables.

16. Underline each word that should be italicized in this sentence: Professor Trinh has published several
(72) interesting articles in our local newspaper, the Mud Valley Gazette.

17. Circle the gerund phrase in this sentence: The Harappas enjoyed living in pleasant mud-brick houses, .
(58)

18. Underline the participial phrase in this sentence and circle the word it modifies: Defending themselves
(59) with large clay missiles, the Harappas survived until about 1700 B.C.

Diagram sentences 19 and 20 in the space to the right.

19. Yesterday, the archeologists dug deep into the ruins
(88, 94) for ancient relics.

20. Future excavating will give us additional
(34, 59) information about the Harappas' daily lives.

Circle the correct word(s) to complete sentences 1–10.

1. The word (real, really) is an adverb.
(92)

2. Down the street (come, comes) two ponies.
(6)

3. The Latin prefix *soli-* means (first, bone, alone).
(99)

4. A multitude is a great (king, many, idea).
(96)

5. The italicized part of this sentence is a(n) (essential, nonessential) part: Anatolia, *which is now called*
(65) *Turkey*, was divided into several kingdoms, each with its own ruler.

6. The italicized part of this sentence is a(n) (noun, adjective, adverb) phrase: *During the period from 2500*
(99) *to 2000 BC,* the Egyptians built more large structures than other people in the Middle East.

7. Only two people in the class, you and (me, I), will make an Egyptian water clock for our display.
(53, 54)

8. A dependent clause may be connected to an independent clause by a (coordinating, subordinating)
(57) conjunction.

9. The following sentence is (simple, compound, complex, compound-complex): Although the people of
(100) Anatolia were among the world's first farmers, they amassed most of their wealth through trading metal.

10. I can't find that information (nowhere, anywhere) in my history book.
(81)

11. Write the comparative form of the adverb *imaginatively*. _____
(90)

12. Circle the conjunctive adverb in this sentence: King Tut had fabulous riches; however, no amount of
(91) wealth could extend his life.

For 13 and 14, circle each letter that should be capitalized, and add punctuation marks as needed.

13. ben said, "hey, grandpa, the exhibit of king tut's tomb is coming to plano, texas, on sunday, november 17,
(44, 46) 2003."

14. moses begged the pharaoh let my people go
(20, 46)

15. Write the possessive form of *Moses*. _____
(97)

16. Underline each word that should be italicized in this sentence: In our entymology textbook, we can read all
(72) about locusts by looking up their scientific name, locusta.

17. Circle the infinitive phrase in this sentence: After the invasion of the Hyksos, the Egyptians learned to use
(96) horses and chariots.

18. In this sentence, underline the participial phrase and circle the word it modifies: Scholars studying
(59) papyrus rolls can learn a great deal about Egyptian life.

Diagram sentences 19 and 20 in the space to the right.

19. In 1503 BC, Queen Hatshepsut became one of the
(39, 94) few women pharoahs.

20. Cooking outside prevented hazardous fires in
(28, 59) Egyptian homes.

Circle the correct word(s) to complete sentences 1–9.

1. José didn't (believe, beleive) my tall tale.
(110)

2. Marta and (he, him) laughed at my fabrication.
(53, 54)

3. The prefix (*trans-, inter-, extra-*) means across.
(109)

4. The prefix *inter-* means (against, between, not).
(108)

5. The italicized part of this sentence is a(n) (essential, nonessential) part: The driver, *Nick*, skillfully
(65) maneuvered the ambulance through the traffic.

6. The italicized part of this sentence is a(n) (noun, adjective, adverb) clause: My grandmother won't do
(99) anything *that might increase her chances of having a stroke*.

7. There were no arguments (between, among) the six teammates.
(95)

8. I haven't (ever, never) seen a roadrunner in this part of the country. Have you?
(81)

9. The following sentence is (simple, compound, complex, compound-complex): Because of a bystander's
(100) screaming for help, the victim had more than one rescuer.

10. Underline the dependent clause and circle the subordinating conjunction in this sentence: Good Samaritan
(57) Laws allow us to protect ourselves legally when we assist ill or injured persons.

11. Write the superlative form of the adverb *imaginatively*. _____
(90)

12. Circle the conjunctive adverb in this sentence: Seek shelter if a thunderstorm approaches; however, if no
(91) shelter is available, get into a car and roll up the windows.

For 13 and 14, circle each letter that should be capitalized, and add punctuation marks as needed.

13. uncontrollable risk factors for stroke are age gender and family history regular exercise reduces one's
(44, 63) chance of stroke, for it increases blood circulation.

14. when you call for help, you should give the dispatcher the victim's location, condition, and name.
(50, 63)

15. Write the possessive form of *roses*. _____
(97)

16. Combine this word and suffix to make a new word: *drop + ed* _____
(108, 109)

17. On the line below, rewrite this sentence using active voice: Angela is surprised by the gift.
(102)

_____

18. Which sentence is clearer? Circle A or B.
(50, 103)
    A. The trailblazer found a downed power line hiking down the path.
    B. Hiking down the path, the trailblazer found a downed power line.

Diagram sentences 19 and 20 in the space to the right.

19. Learning CPR might enable you to save a life.
(59, 96)

20. Now is the time to prepare for a future emergency.
(39, 96)